THE WHOLE SELF LIFESTYLE FOR WORKING PARENTS COMPANION WORKBOOK

A PRACTICAL 4-STEP FRAMEWORK TO DEFEAT BURNOUT AND ESCAPE SURVIVAL MODE FOR GOOD

SARAH ARGENAL, MA, CPC

For permission requests or for reprints or excerpts, contact the publisher at hello@argenalinstitute.com. Our books may be purchased in bulk for promotional, educational, or business use.

ISBN: 978-1-7351254-2-8 (Paperback)

Cover design by Ronald Cruz at www.cruzialdesigns.com.

First Edition: June 2020

Published by The Argenal Institute LLC.

Printed in the United States of America

The Argenal Institute LLC

539 W Commerce St #2091

Dallas, TX 75208

www.argenalinstitute.com

CONTENTS

INTRODUCTION

I had a very two-dimensional view of parenthood before I had kids. I knew becoming a mom would change my life. I understood on a surface-level the logistics of the changes I would go through. I could never have predicted the level of self-discovery, personal growth, and commitment it would take to *enjoy* the journey of parenthood, though. Now I have greater respect for the full-life transformation that takes place when a *parent* is born.

The process of creating a life worth living can be hard and uncomfortable and messy. It can take a long time. It usually includes some uncertainty and pain. It often consists of repetition of life lessons before they "stick." That is why a lot of people, especially working parents who are already overwhelmed, avoid this process. It often seems easier to stay numb to their lives, but then they inadvertently get trapped in a cycle of struggle instead.

The very nature of self-development, of discovering who you are *now* so you can make intentional choices about your life, is the key to finding success, happiness, and growth. It doesn't have to be an intimidating and aversive process. It can be rewarding and deeply meaningful, even if it's accompanied by tears and pain at times. Making lasting changes in life isn't always glamorous, but it's worth the effort.

This workbook will help you defeat burnout in this demanding and unpredictable world so you can finally start *enjoying* your life as a working parent. We're going to bypass the surface-level, one-size-fits-all advice in this book. There's plenty of that out there already. We're going to go deeper. We're going to get more personal. We'll explore the transition you experience on a *molecular* level as you transform from an ambitious professional into a self-confident *working parent*: someone who juggles passion, love, commitment, and perseverance in every area of life without sacrificing one thing over another.

This book holds an invitation to begin living your life from the *inside out*. It encourages you to take actions that will lead to real results, genuine connections, and deep contentment. This book is about living your best life, no matter what that life looks like. I'm not promising it will always be easy. But if you're deliberate, you'll build momentum and the process will become more intuitive over time.

OVERVIEW OF THE WORKBOOK

This workbook edition contains questions, exercises, and resources referenced in The Whole SELF Lifestyle for Working Parents book. If you have somehow come across this Companion Working before reading the book, I would highly recommend stopping here and checking that out first. There are some fundamental principles covered in the book that would be helpful to know before diving into these exercises.

You won't find hot tips or life hacks or shortcuts for happiness in the book. I don't tell you what to do, or how you should live your life. I don't presume to know what your unique combination of challenges are, much less how to fix them. That's for *you* to figure out. Instead, I am here to guide you along that (often baffling) path of self-discovery.

This workbook will offer you a roadmap to build your *own* personal instruction manual for *your* unique experience as a working parent. As you work your way through these exercises, you'll pinpoint the hidden, underlying source of *your* specific struggles. You'll identify your deepest desires and your long-term goals. You'll clarify your individual needs and strengths. You'll get a birds-eye view of the different areas of your life. After you have that big picture perspective of what you're dealing with, then you can dive deep into the areas that require your time and attention in *this* moment.

The prompts in this workbook will help you clarify *your* answers, rather than encourage you to implement anyone else's, including mine. This workbook explores what can happen when you release the fear and commit to doing the hard work of *understanding yourself*. Once you know yourself on a deeper level, you'll learn how to craft a life that finally fits who you are, right now. You'll learn how to stop settling for that toxic cycle of burnout that most modern working parents find themselves trapped in. When you apply the principles outlined in this book, you'll embrace the *real* adventure of working parenthood and all of the treasured moments that await you.

One last note: you'll notice that I tend to use traditional cisgender-specific terms and titles to ease the text flow. I recognize that not everyone will fall into the gender profiles, family structures, or other categories as I outline them. I encourage you to disregard any titles or pronouns that don't fit for you, and update the questions raised in this workbook to best reflect *your* identity.

This book has three distinct parts:

Part 1

In the first part of this workbook, we'll talk about what's causing the burnout epidemic among working parents in modern society. Burnout is occurring everywhere around the world, for a variety of different populations. We'll drill down into the complex combination of reasons why working parents in particular are struggling. You'll get a clearer picture of the full scope of the challenges you face, so you understand what *you're* really dealing with.

Part 2

In the second part of this workbook, you'll work through my signature process, the Whole SELF Lifestyle. This is a proactive approach toward working parenthood that helps you address the logistical and psychological challenges you face as you try to blend work, family, and life in general. You'll create a *personalized* roadmap to understand and improve the essential areas of *your* life. You'll identify the underlying source of your problems, and then customize solutions to those problems that fit who you are today.

Part 3

In the final part of this workbook, you'll discover how you can escape survival mode *for good*. You'll learn how to integrate the principles of the Whole SELF Lifestyle into your daily life on a short- and long-term basis. You'll discover the best circumstances under which the Whole SELF Lifestyle™ framework can be applied, and how you can maintain progress over time.

———

RECOMMENDED RESOURCES

Included at the end of this book is a list of suggested reading materials, podcasts, and links to research and resources that are mentioned throughout this book. A list of these materials is also available in the Bonus Library for ongoing reference.

———

BONUS LIBRARY

I'll be integrating free bonus materials throughout this book, which you are invited to download for free from our **Bonus Library**. These resources will help you go even deeper on your path toward self-discovery. You can access everything in the Bonus Library by going to www.wholeselflifestyle.com/working-parents/bonus-library.

PART I

1

NOT ANOTHER PARENTING ADVICE BOOK

There's no shortage of how-to information for working parents these days. Expert advice is everywhere: Google and Amazon search results, our social media feeds, podcasts, parenting groups, or our parents and siblings and friends. We're inundated with advice and opinions. Self-help is a $11 billion industry full of experts (and not-so-expert novices) who claim they can help you fix all of your problems, usually quickly and easily:

- How to manage your time to make room for what you love.
- How to streamline your morning routine to avoid chaos.
- How to plan a week's worth of meals over the weekend.
- How to discipline your kids when they misbehave.
- How to stay connected with your partner despite sleepless nights, financial stress, and the burden of the mental load.

This is potentially all helpful advice, *if* it happens to work for you. But what about when it *doesn't* work for you? What if you've followed all of these instructions religiously, and you still haven't found relief? What if you've checked off all the boxes that are supposed to lead to happiness, and you still find yourself drowning under the weight of endless obligations, expectations, and responsibilities?

In that case, you may feel like a failure because the clear-cut instruction manuals aren't working for you. You may be thinking: *What's wrong with me? This seems to work for everyone else. I must be doing something wrong. I just need to try a little harder to make it work.*

Nope. You're not the problem.

The advice you receive as a busy working parent in modern society will sometimes be a good fit for you; other times, it won't. It's that simple. That's not a character flaw, it's just a fact.

There are a lot of things in life that are conducive to how-to instructions. Navigating the pitfalls and challenges of modern working parenthood isn't one of them. Working parenthood is complex. It's an "inside job," as the saying goes. It's impossible to design a parenting advice book that will be a perfect fit for *your* unique personality, needs, strengths, and goals in this particular season of your life. There are too many variables to consider. It's impossible for anyone else to tell you what to do or how to do it with any reliability. As much as we want one, there will never be a "one-size fits all" solution for working parenthood.

———

 Everything is either an opportunity to grow or an obstacle to keep you from growing. You get to choose. -Wayne Dyer

———

There are a lot of things in life that are conducive to how-to instructions. Navigating the pitfalls and challenges of modern working parenthood isn't one of them. Working parenthood is complex. It's an "inside job," as the saying goes. It's impossible to design a parenting advice book that will be a perfect fit for *your* unique personality, needs, strengths, and goals in this particular season of your life. There are too many variables to consider. It's impossible for anyone else to tell you what to do or how to do it with any reliability. As much as we want one, there will never be a "one-size fits all" solution for working parenthood.

You won't find hot tips or life hacks or shortcuts for happiness in this book. You won't find my Top 10 Rules for Working Parents, or a list of "secret" tactics to make your life easier. I'm not going to tell you what to do, or how you should live your life. I don't presume to know what your unique combination of challenges are, much less how to fix them. That's for *you* to figure out. Instead, I am here to guide you along that (often baffling) path of self-discovery.

This book will offer you a roadmap to build your *own* personal instruction manual for *your* unique experience as a working parent. As you work your way through this book, you'll pinpoint the hidden, underlying source of *your* specific struggles. You'll identify your deepest desires and your long-term goals. You'll clarify your individual needs and strengths. You'll get a birds-eye view of the different areas of your life. After you have that big picture perspective of what you're dealing with, then you can dive deep into the areas that require your time and attention in *this* moment.

This book will help you clarify *your* answers, rather than encourage you to implement anyone else's, including mine. This book explores what can happen when you release the fear and commit to doing the hard work of *understanding yourself*. Once you know yourself on a deeper level, you'll learn how to craft a life that finally fits who you are, right now. You'll learn how to stop settling for that toxic cycle of burnout that most modern working parents find themselves trapped in. When you apply the principles outlined in this book, you'll embrace the *real* adventure of working parenthood and all of the treasured moments that await you.

2

YOUR JOURNEY OUT OF BURNOUT
STARTS WITH A SMALL STEP

"Burnout" is a word that's tossed around liberally in our society. But I've found that many people don't have a clear view of what burnout is, or how it really impacts their daily lives. I certainly didn't.

The World Health Organization classified "work-related burnout" as a medical phenomenon in 2019. While they don't refer to it as a medical disorder itself, they do acknowledge that burnout produces symptoms that influence people to seek treatment for a variety of other medical disorders, and as a result should be taken into account by medical professionals.

The World Health Organization defines work-related burnout as: *A syndrome conceptualized as resulting from chronic workplace stress that has not been successfully managed. It is characterized by three dimensions:*

- *feelings of energy depletion or exhaustion;*
- *increased mental distance from one's job, or feelings of negativism or cynicism related to one's job; and*
- *reduced professional efficacy.*

While that begins to describe the challenges working parents face, it's woefully incomplete. There were many other symptoms that characterize the burnout experience. Here are some of the more obscure symptoms that often serve as warning signs.

————

 You don't just wake up and become the butterfly. Growth is a process. -Rupi Kour

————

WHICH OF THESE BURNOUT SYMPTOMS DO YOU STRUGGLE WITH?

Physical Symptoms

- Chronic fatigue
- Lack of energy
- Sleep disorders such as over-tiredness or insomnia
- Headaches or migraines
- Distractibility and inability to focus
- Change in appetite leading to extreme weight gain or loss
- Increased illness or weakened immune system
- Chest pains or heart palpitations
- Muscle tension
- Dizziness
- Restlessness

Emotional Symptoms

- Anxiety
- Depression

- Dysthymia (low-level sense of sadness or disinterest in life)
- Overwhelm at common, everyday activities
- Inability to cope with challenging situations
- Guilt
- Anger or rage
- Cynicism or pessimism
- Apathy
- Tearfulness
- Forgetfulness

Relational Symptoms

- Increased conflict with loved ones
- Distancing, detachment, or disconnection
- Impatience with others
- Questioning viability of relationships
- Reduction in effectiveness at home or work
- Isolation
- Lack of trust in others

Lifestyle Symptoms

- Inability to identify and focus on priorities
- Confusion around values and internal purpose
- Doubt about my identity, life purpose, and values
- Poor performance at work or home
- Disorganization
- Loss of productivity
- Loss of motivation
- Powerlessness

How do these symptoms present themselves in your life? What do they look and feel like to you?

_____

_____

_____

_____

_____

_____

_____

_____

_____

_____

_____

_____

_____

_____

_____

_____

_____

_____

_____

_____

_____

_____

_____

_____

3

SELF-CARE CAN'T FIX THIS PROBLEM

The conversation around burnout has been gaining steam over the last few years. It seems that everyone is struggling with a lack of time, exhaustion, and this feeling that their life is all go-go-go. We're aware there's a problem. But the standard solutions aren't making a dent in the issue. In fact, the burnout epidemic seems to be getting worse. We've all heard the advice to focus on self-care to combat those feelings of overwhelm, stress, and exhaustion. We have access to all of the information we could ever need as we search for solutions. Yet most of us are trapped in a vicious cycle of grinding through our endless to-do list until we collapse into bed at night. What are we missing?

———

66 *Growth is uncomfortable because you have never been here before, you've never been this version of you. So give yourself a little grace and breathe through it.* -Kristin Lohr

———

Juggling kids, a demanding career, our relationships, and managing a busy household, we push ourselves in all areas of our lives until we simply can't take on any more. Often, our bodies give out and we get physically ill. Other times we continue on autopilot while we check out of our lives mentally and emotionally. Life feels like a grind, but we power through.

Eventually, we turn to self-care out of necessity. We schedule a massage or an afternoon of golf or plan a date night with our spouse. Sometimes we even escape reality for a whole weekend away. After these short periods of rejuvenation, we return to our normal routine with renewed energy, ready to dive back into the chaos. Within weeks or even days, we're back in survival mode, and the whole process starts all over again.

Over the last few years, self-care has emerged as the key to overcoming burnout in many personal development circles. This well-intentioned advice is being distorted and may be perpetuating the burnout epidemic in our society.

When we're in survival mode, we search for anything that will offer immediate relief from our pain. Self-care can offer that much-needed relief. In that way, it's an important tool. If we're not careful though, we can get stuck in a pattern where we rely on self-care strategies as a Band-Aid solution to escape survival mode without addressing the *source* of our issues. The short-term relief self-care offers can be used as an excuse to avoid examination of the lifestyle issues that caused the burnout in the first place. When we use self-care to dull the pain on a short-term basis, we convince ourselves all is well. We never get around to doing the deeper work of creating a *sustainable* lifestyle over the long term. Until we look beyond our symptoms, self-care strategies just camouflage what's happening under the surface.

Self-care is most effective in two situations: 1) when it's used as a tool to maintain an already healthy lifestyle, and 2) when it's used to energize you long enough for deeper self-reflection so you can integrate long-term changes. If you're using self-care strategies as a temporary solution to escape the depths of burnout, you're doomed to stay trapped in this toxic pattern.

———

What are your favorite self-care strategies to escape burnout?

_____
_____
_____
_____
_____
_____
_____
_____
_____
_____

How do those self-care strategies fit into your regular routine?

_____
_____
_____
_____
_____
_____
_____
_____

4

A HOLISTIC APPROACH

Working parents around the world struggle to reconcile the tension between the different roles we play in our lives. It's easy to feel pulled in a thousand different directions at all times. Whenever we turn our attention to one area of our life, everything else fell apart. Then we have to work overtime to get those other areas of our life back on track, which puts us further behind everywhere else.

As I synthesized my training in all different fields, I began to identify three overlapping systems that appear to operate simultaneously for each of us. All of these systems have a huge impact on our experience of our daily lives. I've also come to think about these different systems in terms of MIND, BODY, and SOUL.

Life Management System
External | Mind

- Childcare
- Work responsibilities
- Home management

- Invisible Labor
- Routines and Systems

The Life Management System refers to all of the different obligations, responsibilities, activities, and pressures you face from *outside* sources. It's your *External System*. This external system often requires a lot of *logistical thinking* and *mental energy* to coordinate. This can include things like meeting work obligations, commitments you've made to your partner, parenting duties, or volunteer projects. They can also include things like household chores or the invisible labor that takes up your time and energy such as scheduling doctor appointments, paying bills, or planning a vacation. Your Life Management System always involves other people; they count on you to meet *their* needs within this system.

Emotional Intelligence System
Internal | Body

- Self-awareness
- Emotional regulation
- Relationships
- Motivation
- Empathy

The Emotional Intelligence System includes the thoughts, feelings, and sensations that are happening within your *body*. This is your *Internal System*. Your emotions, your mental and physical well-being, your habits, your energy levels, your relationships, and your boundaries are all a part of your Emotional Intelligence System. There are times when you may not be in tune with what's happening with this system. This system can feel invisible, since it's not accountable to anyone besides you, and no one else can help you manage it. Your internal system can feel like it exists in the background, but it's a critical part of your experience as a working parent. Sometimes it seems prudent to ignore what's going on internally so you can focus on those external demands that *are* more visible. But if you ignore this system for too long your mental and emotional health starts to break down.

Personal Identity System
Foundational | Soul

- Core values
- Desires and goals
- Unique strengths
- Fears and triggers
- Higher purpose

The Personal Identity System refers to the values, desires, goals, and unique qualities that make you.... *you*. This is your *Foundational System*. This is what makes your life worth living. This is your *soul in action*. These are the fundamental principles, beliefs, and personality traits that guide your life experience. Your personal identity guides your actions, ideas, perspectives, and insights. The more in touch you are with who you are on a foundational basis, the more you can utilize that deep inner awareness to create a life you love.

———

66 *You're not stuck. You're just committed to certain patterns of behavior because they helped you in the past. Now those behaviors have become more harmful than helpful.* -Emily Marontian

———

FLIP THE FOCUS

SARAH ARGENAL, MA, CPC

Most working parents who struggle with burnout are often living from the *outside in*. They get bombarded with *external* demands, and all of their time, energy, and focus go into meeting those external demands first and foremost. They are so focused on the Life Management System of their life that the Emotional Intelligence and Personal Identity Systems take a backseat. The problem with this approach is that the Emotional Intelligence and Personal Identity Systems are the source of *meaning* in our lives: our relationships, our ambitions, what gives us energy, how we feel about ourselves, our very sense of *who we are*. When we neglect those systems, we lose control over our experience.

When working parents become consumed with external demands, their Emotional Intelligence System goes haywire under the surface. They feel stressed, depressed, disconnected, and anxious, but they're too busy to pinpoint why. They don't take the time to address their *emotional* or *interpersonal* needs, so their life spirals out of control.

When working parents lose touch with their Personal Identity System, they feel disconnected from their *current* core values: their deepest desires, how they've grown into parenthood, and what they want from their career now. They "feel different," but haven't had time to explore *how* their identity has changed, or how it guides their choices, behaviors, and beliefs in each moment.

Most working parents aren't managing any of these systems intentionally. They're too busy. Everything runs on autopilot, which results in reacting to the most urgent emergency without taking into account how their reaction will impact the system *as a whole*.

Here's the truth we all intuitively know; blending all of these systems in a fulfilling way is not going to happen by accident. We need to reclaim control of our lives and manage each of these systems *deliberately*. The framework in Part 2 of this workbook will help you get a sense of all of the different systems that are operating in *your* life right now. You can start to shine a light on some of the outdated beliefs, assumptions, behaviors, or parts of your identity that may not serve you anymore.

———

Do you feel like you're living from the outside, in? How connected do you feel to your Emotional Intelligence and Personal Identity Systems today? Where do you feel disconnected?

PART II

5

THE WHOLE SELF LIFESTYLE™ PHILOSOPHY

T he Whole SELF Lifestyle is a *philosophy* as well as a practical *framework* to help working parents address the logistical and psychological challenges they face as they try to blend work, family, and life in general. It gives working parents a customized roadmap to escape survival mode on their own terms. We'll cover the philosophy of the Whole SELF Lifestyle in this chapter, and then move on to how the framework breaks down in the next chapter.

The Philosophy

The Whole SELF Lifestyle philosophy offers an alternative to the hustle-and-grind culture that's taking over our society right now. It encourages dedicated professionals to make the most of their lives without sacrificing what matters most to them. This approach is about creating a lifestyle that works for *you*, based on your unique strengths, needs, desires, circumstances, and goals. And as a busy working parent, you need a flexible system that can work within the various constraints of your life.

___

 Go where there is no path and leave a trail. -Einstein

___

THE 3 PILLARS OF THE WHOLE SELF LIFESTYLE

There are three main components of the Whole SELF Lifestyle that all work together simultaneously.

Pillar #1: Whole

We, as human beings, are meant to feel *whole*. As working parents, we're always fielding demands and pressure from the outside world. Being in reaction mode to all of these different areas of our lives can make us feel scattered, stretched thin, depleted, and resentful. I often hear working parents using these phrases to describe their experience trying to stay on top of everything they manage on a day-to-day basis:

- *I don't have enough time.*
- *Balance isn't possible.*
- *I never have enough energy.*
- *I'm drowning.*
- *I can't keep up.*
- *I'm failing at everything.*
- *My to-do list is a mile long.*
- *I'll take care of myself when things slow down.*

Many of the obligations we face are indeed important. We can't just ignore them. But others could potentially be put on the back burner for a while. Others really could be dismissed indefinitely without any major consequences. But until you take the time to critically evaluate everything that's coming at you from the outside world, it will be difficult to make informed decisions about your life. The Whole SELF Lifestyle helps you integrate all of the different areas of your life into one functioning whole.

Pillar #2: Self

Becoming a parent has a way of shattering everything we thought we knew about ourselves. Our identity goes through a significant transformation, a deepening. We inevitably surrender old parts of ourselves. We take on new roles in our relationships and our lives. We start to understand ourselves in different ways. We face all sorts of new circumstances, which require new skills and perspectives to adapt to. We try to blend who we used to be with who we are becoming. But so many working parents today are too busy to explore this shifting identity in any useful way. I often hear working parents use phrases like:

- *I don't know who I am anymore.*
- *I've lost myself.*
- *I miss who I used to be.*
- *I don't know what to do.*
- *I feel so guilty.*
- *I'm unhappy.*
- *There has to be more to life than this.*

When we're not clear about our inner world, we become increasingly persuaded by outside influences. We rely on experts and "gurus" and opinions of friends and family. This reliance on external sources for wisdom leads to a loss of confidence to do what's best for ourselves, our families, and our future. Our sense of self, as a result, isn't understood deeply enough to guide our choices, behavior, or beliefs in a meaningful way. We're living from the outside in, which is backward. When this happens, it's easy to find ourselves living out other people's agendas and values rather than our own. This is what makes life as a working parent feel like a grind, an endless loop of non-stop responsibilities. The Whole SELF Lifestyle helps you go through a process of self-discovery that honors the different parts of who *you* are so you can approach every situation you encounter with a solid sense of *self*. It gives you confidence that the choices you make are right for *you*.

Pillar #3: Lifestyle

The third part of this philosophy is all about establishing a healthy *lifestyle*. Creating a fulfilling life is not a destination. It's not an outcome. It's not something to achieve. It's a *practice*. It's an ongoing discipline. It's a way of being in the world. It will fluctuate. Some days you'll be better at it than others. As long as you get clear about who you are and keep your intentions top of mind, the demands of daily life won't pull you off track as easily. And when you *do* get pulled off track, you'll know how to course-correct quickly. The Whole SELF Lifestyle helps you replace the constant searching for answers outside of yourself with a *reliable* and *repeatable* process that will support you in discovering the right answers for you in each season of your life.

The 3 pillars of the Whole SELF Lifestyle remind us to stay grounded within our *whole self* as we move through the chaos that comes with working parenthood. It helps us explore our old, unconscious patterns of behavior, understand those patterns on a deeper level, and make healthier choices going forward. It's a way to up-level the baseline of our thoughts, beliefs, perspectives, decisions, behaviors, and experiences. Over time, we gradually improve our lives in every area.

PUTTING THE WHOLE SELF LIFESTYLE INTO PRACTICE

The next four chapters will explore the Whole SELF Lifestyle *framework*, which breaks down the Whole SELF Lifestyle philosophy into four distinct action-oriented steps. You'll find a series of self-reflection questions, exercises, and prompts to help you understand yourself and the circumstances of your life on a deeper level. These are questions you can start answering one by one today. It doesn't require a huge life change. You are encouraged to begin with small steps to avoid overwhelm. The key is that you're looking at the big picture of your life. From there, you can make strategic choices about all areas of your life.

6

THE WHOLE SELF LIFESTYLE™ FRAMEWORK

The Whole SELF Lifestyle framework helps busy working parents break the abstract philosophy down into concrete steps in their own lives. This 4-step framework offers a holistic guide to help you understand not only the surface-level symptoms you're feeling in your life, but also the *real* source of your struggles within the context of a more extensive system.

By breaking things down and starting from where you are now, you're able to make manageable but immediate changes that will give you back the time, energy, and focus you need to continue to make more changes over time. These small changes will impact the broader ecosystem of your entire life. Instead of scrambling to find the next "silver bullet" solution to your problems, or numbing out because you can't manage your life anymore, you'll start crafting the lifestyle that works for *you*, in *this* season of your life. It's all done in a strategic way that provides some much-needed clarity and peace now, but also keeps in mind the longer-term vision you have for your life.

I use the acronym S.E.L.F. to break down the Whole SELF Lifestyle philosophy into a practical four-step process.

STEP 1: (S) SYSTEM INVENTORY

Our lives are made up of a complex series of internal and external systems that operate simultaneously. The more efficient each part of these systems is, and the more they're designed to operate in congruence with each other, the happier and healthier we feel in our lives – the more *whole* we are. The first step of the Whole SELF Lifestyle framework is to complete an inventory of the different systems that are operating in your unique life so you can use *that* reality as a starting point for lasting change.

STEP 2: (E) EVALUATE

Once you have identified the different systems that are currently active in your life, it's time to evaluate each one to see what's working for you and what isn't. You also analyze how all of the systems are working together in your life. Then you decide what you want your life to look like – your ideal. Once you've analyzed these systems, and how things are working together, then you can identify what needs to happen to get from where you currently are to where you want to go.

STEP 3: (L) LIST OF SOLUTIONS

The first two steps of the Whole SELF Lifestyle framework provide clarity and a roadmap for change. Now you're in a position to brainstorm the action steps that will improve different areas of your life. This is when it's helpful to do research, listen to podcasts, read books, get advice, etc. Then you can make an educated decision about your next steps. Doing the first two steps of this framework limits overwhelm and bright shiny object syndrome, and allows you to focus on the best next steps for you in this moment of your life.

STEP 4: (F) FAMILIARIZE

In this final step, you *implement* and *experiment*. You try out different action steps you brainstormed in the last step. You decide what really works for you, your family, your career, and your life – and what doesn't. You discard what doesn't work, and you repeat what does work so it becomes a new habit in your life. You refine and evolve based on what you learn. Over time, you familiarize yourself with new ways of being in the world, new habits, new routines, and a more satisfying lifestyle that's centered around your *whole self*.

———

❝❝ Get in the habit of asking yourself: 'Does this support the life I'm trying to create?' -Well Doctor

———

This action-oriented process allows you to start big and broad to get a big-picture perspective of your life. Then once you have a clear high-level view of what's happening in your life, you can make informed decisions to drill down into the areas of your life that need the most attention. The result will be long-term changes based on a clear understanding of who you really are, what you really need, what you really want, and the best way forward in your current circumstances.

We're going to expand your vantage point so that you can make more informed choices. Knowing where to focus your time, energy, and attention will alleviate the guilt, second-guessing, and shiny object syndrome that plagues many working parents. When you make a choice, *any* choice, you'll know exactly why. You'll have a broader perspective, and you'll understand how changes in one area of your life might impact all of the others because you've consciously thought it through.

Once you've gone through the Whole SELF Lifestyle framework once, you can use it as a tool over and over again in your life. You can repeat these steps whenever you're feeling burned out, or when a significant life shift happens, or if you're just craving an upgrade in the quality of your life. You can apply this methodology to any situation in your life. You can also use this methodology on a broad basis to examine every area of your life, or you can zoom in on trouble areas to get more immediate and specific relief.

Self-discovery happens, and can *only* happen, if you go through *all four* of these steps. Most people today spend all of their time in the third step, ignoring all of the other stages of the growth process. Accumulating information indiscriminately and failing to put anything into action contributes to those feelings of overwhelm, failure, and guilt since you're just consuming information without any strategy, direction, or purpose to put it into practice.

HOW TO APPLY THIS FRAMEWORK

Go through the questions in the next four chapters to explore the systems that are currently consuming *your* time, energy, and attention. You may be tempted to ignore the next few chapters. It may seem overwhelming, or just too much to dive into right now. It's okay to gloss over the questions now, finish the book, and then come back to dive into the exercises later. But know that the *real* transformation you're looking for comes from answering these questions, and then integrating the insight you gain into your daily life. You don't have to do it all in one sitting (please, don't!). Take your time. Do it at your own pace. But do follow these general guidelines to get the most out of this process (and your life).

1. **Answer each question honestly.** The more honest you are in your responses, the more impact you'll feel. Remember, no one else will see your answers besides you (unless you want them to), so get *real*.
2. **Avoid self-judgment.** Don't assign a label of "good" or

"bad" to any of your answers. Think of yourself as a neutral observer as you answer these questions.

3. **Be brief.** Don't feel compelled to write several pages per answer (unless you want to!). The goal here is to provide clarity for yourself in a variety of areas in your life. Your answers can start with a short overview based on what immediately comes to mind for you. Give yourself permission to touch on the most important parts of each answer. A few sentences will do. When something striking arises, feel free to get more in-depth on those questions, if you're inspired to do so.

4. **Give yourself time.** Don't feel like you have to answer all of these questions in one sitting. Focus on a handful of questions at a time, and then give yourself a break. Self-reflection can be mentally and emotionally draining, and there's no need to rush through this process. Remember, this is a *lifestyle*, not a quick fix. There will also probably be times when you're in the "flow" and are motivated to keep going. That's okay too! Just follow your instincts without judgment, and you'll get through it at the perfect time.

5. **Be compassionate with yourself.** The tendency when you complete these exercises is to focus on everything that needs to be "fixed." But don't forget to identify what you do *well* too! We are all a mix of strengths and weaknesses. Be honest but be fair to yourself also. Avoid the temptation to be overly critical.

6. **Allow your responses to change.** You are a living, breathing human. Your life circumstances are changing moment to moment. The lessons you learn accumulate over time, which will change your perspective and needs. Use that information to refresh your responses as needed. As I write this book, most of the world is under a stay-at-home lockdown order to avoid spreading the coronavirus

disease. The answers you come up with in that situation are going to vary greatly from the responses that come up when life is relatively normal. That's okay. Let this be a living document that reflects wherever you are *today*.

———

BONUS LIBRARY

I've prepared a handful of bonus materials to help you dive deeper into the following exercises. You can access these bonus materials in **The Whole SELF Lifestyle™ Bonus Library** here: www.wholeselflifestyle.com/working-parents/bonus-library.

7

STEP 1: (S) SYSTEM INVENTORY

T he first step of the Whole SELF Lifestyle framework is "**S**," for **System Inventory**. The System Inventory is a critical part of the Whole SELF Lifestyle. Without a clear understanding of all of the different micro-systems that make up your life, you'll continue to feel like you're *reacting* to your life. This process of identifying the details of the systems in your life will set the foundation for the rest of our work.

Answer these questions as they apply to you *today*. You may feel tempted to skip the questions that don't seem "relevant" or that aren't causing you the most difficulty right now. Avoid the temptation to skip any questions. We often discover hidden treasures in the least likely places. It's also important to get the broadest perspective possible. You may be surprised at what comes up for you or how different areas of your life are connected when you explore all of the nooks and crannies of your life.

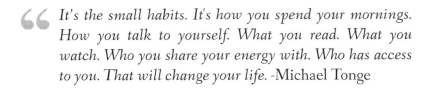

It's the small habits. It's how you spend your mornings. How you talk to yourself. What you read. What you watch. Who you share your energy with. Who has access to you. That will change your life. -Michael Tonge

———

SELF-INQUIRY QUESTIONS

*You can access the **System Inventory Snapshot** in the **Bonus Library** at www.wholeselflifestyle.com/working-parents/bonus-library.*

———

Life Management System
External | Mind

This section relates to all of the ***external***, ***logistical*** aspects of your life as a working parent.

Family

Who is in your immediate, nuclear family (spouse/part-ner, kids, pets)?

Who is in your extended family (parents, grandparents, siblings, aunts, uncles, cousins, in-laws, etc.)?

Career and Purpose

What is the role of your career in your life right now?

What is your primary job or source of income?

Do you have any side projects that you're working on? If so, what does that entail?

Are you dedicating your time to any volunteer pursuits? Describe.

What other passions or hobbies are you currently focused on?

Are there any other contributions you're making in your career or to fulfill a deeper purpose in your life?

_____

_____

_____

_____

_____

_____

_____

What are your professional goals for the future? One year from now? Five years from now? Ten years from now?

_____

_____

_____

_____

_____

_____

_____

_____

_____

_____

_____

_____

_____

_____

Household Management

How does the role of household management factor into your life right now?

_____
_____
_____
_____
_____
_____
_____
_____
_____

How do you feel about the current state of your home environment?

_____
_____
_____
_____
_____
_____
_____
_____
_____

How organized are you, in general?

_____
_____
_____
_____

How do household chores currently get done at your home?

How do you maintain a functional and organized space? Who else is involved in maintaining your home?

Systems and Processes

Who handles your family schedule?

How do you keep your work, family, and other obligations organized? Do you have a to-do list? A family calendar?

How do you organize your mail and paperwork? What happens to those items when they come in?

_____

_____

_____

_____

_____

_____

_____

_____

How do you manage your finances and bills? Do you have a budgeting system?

_____

_____

_____

_____

_____

What's your system for organizing, signing, and returning school paperwork?

_____

_____

_____

_____

_____

_____

_____

How do you maintain important papers (wills, marriage licenses, birth certificates, marriage certificates, etc.)?

How do you plan for and prepare meals? Breakfast? Lunch? Dinner? Snacks? Weekdays? Weekends?

Who is currently responsible for carpool and supervising after-school activities?

Who handles errands in your home?

Childcare

Who is responsible for feeding your kids? Breakfast? Lunch? Dinner? Snacks? Weekday? Weekend?

Who handles getting the kids dressed every day?

SARAH ARGENAL, MA, CPC

How do you manage the supervision of your children?

How do you feel about your kids' education right now?

Who is involved in the cognitive, moral, and social and emotional development of your family? How does that development usually happen?

Mental Load

How does vacation research generally happen in your family?

_____
_____
_____
_____
_____
_____
_____

How are doctor's appointments scheduled? For the kids? For you? For your partner?

_____
_____
_____
_____
_____
_____
_____

How are school supplies prepared and packed each day? Packing backpacks, extra clothes, diapers, lunch, bottles, etc.?

_____
_____
_____
_____
_____
_____

47

How do you hire and supervise other workers in your home (nannies, housekeepers, assistants, dog walkers, etc.)?

_____
_____
_____
_____
_____
_____

Who takes care of your pets if you have any? What does that entail?

_____
_____
_____
_____
_____
_____

How are major life transitions handled in your family (big moves, job changes, new baby, new school years, etc.)?

_____
_____
_____
_____
_____
_____
_____

How do you handle 401(k), life insurance, car insurance management? Who is generally responsible for management of these types of financial accounts?

_____

_____

_____

_____

_____

_____

_____

_____

What other activities and responsibilities do you think about regularly that weren't listed?

_____

_____

_____

_____

_____

_____

_____

_____

———

The **Family Management Plan** in the **Bonus Library** will help you identify the full range of household management and invisible labor required in your daily life. Access it here now: www. wholeselflifestyle.com/working-parents/bonus-library.

———

Routines

How do you manage your morning routine right now?

_____

_____

_____

_____

_____

_____

_____

_____

What's involved in your evening routine?

_____

_____

_____

_____

_____

_____

_____

How do you manage the kids' school or daycare schedules right now?

_____

_____

_____

_____

_____

_____

What is involved in your current work schedule and demands? Do you have any excessive stress related to work right now? Describe.

How do you fit exercise into your schedule right now? What fitness activities do you enjoy doing most?

What kind of spiritual practice do you integrate into your day? Meditations, prayer, church, journaling?

Family, Friends, and Social Events

How much time do you need alone to re-charge?

How much time do you need with others to re-charge?

How do you integrate time to recharge into your daily routine right now?

How do you decide when to spend time with your spouse right now? What does that time together usually include?

When do you usually get to spend quality time with your close friends? What does that typically look like for you?

How do you decide which social activities to commit to?

Organization

Digital: How do you organize your digital life (mobile device, computer, etc.)?

_____

_____

_____

_____

_____

_____

_____

Time: How do you make decisions about your time?

_____

_____

_____

_____

_____

_____

_____

Physical: How do you stay organized at home? At work? In your car? In other areas of your life?

_____

_____

_____

_____

_____

_____

_____

What did I miss?

What other areas are you focusing on that I didn't list above?

_____
_____
_____
_____
_____
_____
_____

What other obligations do you have right now?

_____
_____
_____
_____
_____
_____

What other systems or routines are a big part of your life right now?

_____
_____
_____
_____
_____
_____
_____

Emotional Intelligence System
Internal | Body

This section relates to all of the *internal*, *psychological*, and *relational* aspects of your life as a working parent.

Self-Awareness

How often do you do self-development work?

_____
_____
_____
_____
_____
_____
_____
_____

How often do you find yourself feeling disconnected from who you are, deep down?

_____
_____
_____
_____
_____
_____
_____
_____
_____

How well do you feel you know yourself right now?

How do you stay in tune with yourself generally throughout the day?

Do you have a mindfulness practice right now? If so, what does that involve?

Mental Health

How do you support your mental health?

How does your mental health impact your experience of the world?

What do you need to do to be at your healthiest, mentally?

Physical Health

How do you support your physical health?

How does your physical health impact your experience of the world?

What do you need to be at your best physically?

Emotional Health

How do you support your emotional health?

How does your emotional health impact your experience of the world?

What do you need to be at your best emotionally?

Motivation

When do you feel most motivated?

What personal goals do you have for yourself right now?

What professional goals do you have for yourself right now?

What do you feel your eternal life purpose is?

How do you integrate habits into your life to ensure you get what you want?

Do you have any bad habits in your life you'd like to change? How would you like those habits to be different?

Energy

Where do you get your energy?

_____

_____

_____

_____

_____

_____

_____

What gives you energy? What activities? Which people?

_____

_____

_____

_____

_____

_____

What depletes your energy? Which activities? Which people?

_____

_____

_____

_____

_____

_____

_____

When are you usually the most focused? What time of day? What are the circumstances?

When do you usually go into "auto-pilot" mode, when you're in motion, but not particularly conscious about what you're doing?

What role does recreation and hobbies play in your life?

What hobbies did you enjoy before parenthood?

Which of those hobbies do you miss? Which would you like to integrate into your life today?

What makes you feel complete?

When do you feel most in the "flow" (happy, entirely focused on what you're doing, with no distractions)?

What do you wish you had more time to do?

What activities do you most enjoy now?

If time wasn't a factor, what would you do more of?

What activities are a "part" of you? Which can't you do without?

What do you do purely for fun?

Marriage and Committed Partnerships

What is the role of marriage or committed partnerships in your life right now?

What were the qualities that attracted you to your partner when you first met them?

What are your favorite qualities about your partner now?

Who were your biggest relationship influences throughout your life?

Who were your partner's biggest relationship influences?

What are your biggest strengths as a couple?

How do you and your partner handle conflict?

_____

_____

_____

_____

_____

_____

_____

What is your primary role in your marriage?

_____

_____

_____

_____

_____

_____

_____

_____

Your partner's primary role in your marriage?

_____

_____

_____

_____

_____

_____

_____

_____

How do you and your partner handle co-parenting?

What do you do for fun together?

How do you support each other as individuals?

How do you divide household management?

How do you divide the invisible labor?

What are you most satisfied with in your relationship right now?

What are you least satisfied with in your relationship right now?

_____
_____
_____
_____
_____
_____
_____

How do you spend your free time together?

_____
_____
_____
_____
_____
_____
_____

Relationship with Your Kids

What is your role as a parent?

_____
_____
_____
_____
_____
_____
_____
_____

What is your partner's role as a parent? How is this role different from yours?

What were the biggest parenting influences from your childhood?

What were your partner's biggest parenting influences from their childhood?

How are your kids unique as people? What are their most defining traits?

What are your biggest strengths as a parent?

What are your partner's biggest strengths as a parent?

How do you connect best with your kids?

How do you integrate spending quality time together as a family into your week?

How do you adapt to new ages, stages, and changes as your kids grow?

How do you deal with challenging behaviors?

What's most important to you as a parent? What is your primary purpose as a parent, if you had to choose one?

Extended Family

Who is in your family of origin? Who did you grow up with?

Parents

Siblings

Blended family members

Who are the grandparents in your life?

Who are the aunts, uncles, and cousins in your life?

What is the role of extended family in your life?

In-Laws and Co-Parents

Who are your parents-in-law?

Who are your siblings-in-law?

Blended in-law family members, if any?

Do you have any ex-partners or co-parents in your life? Who are they?

Do you have any adoptive family members?

Who else is in your family? Did I miss anyone? Add them here.

Friendships and Community

What is the role of friendships in your life?

Who are your closest friends? What do you love most about them?

Who are your oldest friends? How have you stayed in each other's lives all these years?

Who are your professional friends?

Who are your neighbors?

Who are your more distant acquaintances?

What other community contacts do you have in your life right now?

Empathy and Compassion

How do you escape the natural limits of your own perspective? How do you open yourself to what other people are experiencing?

How are you able to see things from another's point of view?

Do you feel comfortable sitting in silence with someone who is struggling?

How do you best provide support to your loved ones who need it?

How do you feel about offering empathy (bringing up your own emotions to connect with someone else) or sympathy (feeling pity for someone else) who is struggling?

Are you able to accept others for who they are without trying to change them?

How do you cope with other people's struggles and big emotions?

Big Feelings

How aware are you of the negative and positive feelings you experience?

What is causing you anxiety right now? What are you afraid will happen in the future?

What is causing you sadness or grief right now? What are you missing from the past? What lifts your spirits?

How do you handle overwhelming feelings? What works for you to navigate, process, and overcome those feelings?

How do you integrate joy and peace into your daily life?

What holds you back from leaning into your big feelings?

———

Personal Identity System
Foundational | Soul

This section relates to all of the **foundational**, **non-negotiable** aspects of your life as a working parent.

Identity

What is your overall understanding of who you are?

How has your view of yourself changed over the last five years? The last ten years?

How can you integrate a regular practice into your life to refresh your view of yourself over time?

What are some of the most prominent defining characteristics of your identity today? What makes you... you?

Values

Check out the **Values & Priorities Profile** exercise in the **Bonus Library** to help with this section. You can access it here now: www.wholeselflifestyle.com/working-parents/bonus-library.

What are your <u>Current Values</u>? What's most important to you on a fundamental level right now?

What are your <u>Aspirational Values</u>? What are you striving for in your life?

Core Beliefs

What are some of the most notable stories you heard as a child?

_____
_____
_____
_____
_____
_____
_____

What is your perspective on the world, based on your life experience?

_____
_____
_____
_____
_____
_____
_____

What is one of your most firm beliefs about life, relationships, success, or happiness?

_____
_____
_____
_____
_____
_____
_____

When is the first time you remember believing this? Describe the situation.

How does this belief show up in your life today?

What do you get out of believing this now? What's the payoff for you?

Are you making any assumptions that may not be true?

What do you know for sure?

What drives you? What are you confident about in your life today?

Accomplishments

Which accomplishments (personal or professional) are you most proud of?

What allowed you to achieve those things?

What do you believe was the key to your being able to achieve those things?

How do you feel about claiming credit or pride in your accomplishments? How does it feel to you?

Personality Traits

What are some of your best personality traits?

Which personality traits would you like to develop, improve, or change?

What's the flip side of that personality trait? How can you express that trait in a healthier way?

Which personality traits do you wish you didn't have? What could those parts of yourself be trying to protect you from?

Life Vision

What did you want your life to look like when you were younger?

What's the most recent life vision you had for yourself?

Take a breath. Get focused on who you are now. What would you like your life to look like in one year? In three years? In ten years?

How has your life vision changed since the last time you've asked yourself this question? How have you changed?

What are your goals in these areas of your life?

Career and Purpose

Family

Self

Regrets

Do you have any regrets in your life? If so, what's your biggest regret in your life so far?

Have you been able to forgive yourself for this regret? If not, why not?

Have you been able to forgive anyone else who may have been involved? If not, why not?

What have you learned from these experiences that you have (or can) integrate into future experiences?

Have you been able to move on from these regrets in your life, or do they hold you back today?

If they're still holding you back, how does that look in your day to day life?

_____

_____

_____

_____

_____

_____

_____

Triggers

What are some of your biggest triggers?

_____

_____

_____

_____

_____

_____

_____

Negative Triggers: What triggers you to behave in ways you don't want to?

_____

_____

_____

_____

_____

Positive Triggers: What helps you behave in ways you want to?

Are there any experiences or stories that others share that create difficulty for you?

What reminds you of negative past experiences?

What motivates you to act when you don't want to?

Fears and Insecurities

What are some of your biggest fears? What are you most afraid of today?

Do you notice any particular insecurities about yourself? What do you wish you could hide from others?

How do those fears or insecurities currently hold you back from living the type of life you want?

Do you know where these fears or insecurities originated?

Perceived Strengths

What do you believe are your biggest strengths today? In what ways are you awesome?

How did you develop those strengths?

_____

_____

_____

_____

_____

_____

_____

_____

How can you build on these strengths in your life?

_____

_____

_____

_____

_____

_____

_____

_____

How do these strengths contribute to your life?

_____

_____

_____

_____

_____

_____

_____

Perceived Weaknesses

What do you believe are your most limiting weaknesses right now?

_____
_____
_____
_____
_____
_____
_____

What do you struggle with the most?

_____
_____
_____
_____
_____
_____
_____

How do you feel about these weaknesses? Are you actively trying to improve them, or do you accept them?

_____
_____
_____
_____
_____
_____

Do you __want__ to improve these weaknesses? If not, why not?

Treasured Moments

What are your most treasured moments to this day?

What do those moments mean to you? How do they contribute to your overall understanding of yourself?

Are you able to share these moments with others in your life? Why or why not?

What types of circumstances led to these treasured moments?

Do you see a pattern among your most treasured moments (i.e., what do you look back on in your life with the most fondness and love)?

Are you able to craft a life that will improve your chances of collecting more treasured moments?

When you look back on your life, what do you believe will be the moments you remember most?

Spirituality and Connection

What is the role of spirituality in your life today?

Do you have a religious or spiritual practice (church, meditation, retreats, journaling, etc.)?

What are your most effective self-reflection practices?

How do you connect with society on a larger scale? How do you get out of your head and develop meaning in your life?

How do you make time to connect to your higher power, or to something greater than yourself (if you're not spiritual)?

_____

_____

_____

_____

_____

_____

_____

NEXT STEPS

Whew! You did it! I know that was a lot of questions. I hope you took some time between the questions to gather your energy and to reflect as you needed to.

Now you have some real, *current* data to work with. In the next chapter, we're going to do some analysis to identify where you can make some changes and start to enjoy this working parenthood journey.

BONUS RECAP

You can find these bonus materials in our **Bonus Library** at: www.wholeselflifestyle.com/working-parents/bonus-library.

- **System Inventory Snapshot**
- **Family Management Plan**
- **Values & Priorities Profile**

8

STEP 2: (E) EVALUATE

The second step of the Whole SELF Lifestyle framework is "**E**," for **Evaluate**.

Now that you have a clear idea of the different micro-systems that are operating in your life right now, it's time to analyze those systems, first independently and then as a whole, to determine what's working well and what could be working better. Answer these questions for each system to identify the areas where you can focus your time and energy to make the most intentional changes in your life.

You don't need to know how you'll make these changes yet. That'll come in the next step. For now, you're just pin-pointing the things that you would like to change. Try not to judge or edit your answers to these questions. Make a laundry list of the things that you *like* about this area of your life, and the things you want to *improve* or work on. I know it can seem impossible to fix whatever struggles you're facing in these areas, but it's worth assessing the different areas of your life without getting pulled immediately into problem-solving mode.

You also don't have to look at your entire life all at once. That can feel overwhelming, especially in the beginning. You can start by focusing on just one area of your life. Some people start with the area that's causing them the most stress, where they need immediate relief. Other people start with an area that's meaningful for them, such as their relationship with their kids or spouse. Other people focus on an area that will make it easier to work on the *other* areas, like managing their energy or mental health. Once you have all of the different areas of your life laid out in front of you on paper from the first step, it's a lot easier to make some educated decisions about where to drill down to focus your efforts.

———

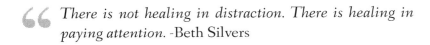 *There is not healing in distraction. There is healing in paying attention.* -Beth Silvers

———

EVALUATE

*You can access the **Evaluate Checklist** in the **Bonus Library** at:* www.wholeselflifestyle.com/working-parents/bonus-library.

———

Life Management System
External | Mind

Out of all of the **Life Management** areas you identified in the last chapter, which 3 systems feel *least* satisfying for you right now? Which areas do you want to prioritize first? List them in order of priority.

1. _____
2. _____
3. _____

If you had to focus on *one* area to improve first, which of these systems do you feel compelled to work on first? This can be the area you identified as being least satisfying to you, but it may also be an area that you've been wanting to improve for a while, or an area you think will improve the others. Which area would you like to focus on first?

————

LIFE MANAGEMENT SYSTEM: *List your **top** priority here for easy reference.*

_____
_____
_____

————

Emotional Intelligence System
Internal | Body

Out of all of the **Emotional Intelligence** areas you identified in the last chapter, which 3 systems feel *least* satisfying for you right now? Which areas do you want to prioritize in our work now? List them in order of priority.

1. _____
2. _____
3. _____

If you had to focus on *one* area to improve first, which of these systems do you feel compelled to work on first? This can be the area you identified as being least satisfying to you, but it may also be an area that you've been wanting to improve for a while, or an area you think will improve the others. Which area would you like to focus on first?

————

EMOTIONAL INTELLIGENCE SYSTEM: *List your **top** priority here for easy reference.*

——
——
——

————

Personal Identity System
Foundational | Soul

Out of all of the **Personal Identity** areas you identified in the last chapter, which 3-5 systems feel *least* satisfying for you right now? Which areas do you want to prioritize in our work now? List them in order of priority.

1. ————————————————————————————————————
2. ————————————————————————————————————
3. ————————————————————————————————————

If you had to focus on *one* area to improve first, which of these systems do you feel compelled to work on first? This can be the area you identified as being least satisfying to you, but it may also be an area that you've been wanting to improve for a while, or an area you think will improve the others. Which area will you focus on first?

———

PERSONAL IDENTITY SYSTEM: *List your **top** priority here for easy reference.*

_____
_____
_____

———

LIFE MANAGEMENT SYSTEM

Answer the self-reflections questions below as they relate to the **Life Management Priorities** you listed above.

LIFE MANAGEMENT SYSTEM: *Copy your top priority from above.*

_____
_____
_____

Past

What actions or beliefs seem to be a pattern in this area of your life?

_____
_____
_____
_____
_____
_____

_____
_____
_____
_____
_____
_____

How did these beliefs or patterns become a part of your routine?

_____
_____
_____
_____
_____
_____
_____
_____
_____

What benefits were you getting from this behavior then? How was it serving you?

_____
_____
_____
_____
_____
_____
_____
_____
_____
_____

Present

What are you getting from this now?

How has this become a habit for you in your current life? How does it manifest now?

How is this working for you in these areas of your life?

Physically

Mentally

Emotionally

Spiritually

How is this <u>not</u> working for you in these areas of your life?

Physically

Mentally

Emotionally

Spiritually

Do your actions and beliefs in this area align with your current values?

Which SELF sub-personality parts are showing up for you?

_____
_____
_____
_____

How are these parts holding you back right now?

_____
_____
_____
_____
_____
_____

How are these actions or beliefs impacting this part of the system?

_____
_____
_____
_____
_____

How are these actions or beliefs impacting other parts of the system?

_____
_____
_____
_____
_____

What do you want to <u>stop</u> doing in this area of your life?

What do you want to <u>start</u> doing in this area of your life?

What do you want to <u>continue</u> doing in this area of your life?

Future

What do you want this area of your life to look like?

_____
_____
_____
_____
_____
_____
_____
_____

In a perfect world, how would it feel?

_____
_____
_____
_____
_____
_____

What questions do you still have about this area of your life?

_____
_____
_____
_____
_____
_____
_____

How would a change impact your life, for better or for worse?

Emotional Intelligence System
Internal | Body

Answer the self-reflections questions below as they relate to the **Emotional Intelligence Priorities** you listed above.

EMOTIONAL INTELLIGENCE SYSTEM: *Copy your top priority from above.*

_____
_____
_____

Past

What actions or beliefs seem to be a pattern in this area of your life?

_____
_____
_____
_____
_____
_____
_____
_____
_____
_____
_____
_____
_____

How did these beliefs or patterns become a part of your routine?

What benefits were you getting from this behavior then? How was it serving you?

Present

What are you getting from this now?

How has this become a habit for you, in your current life? How does it manifest now?

How is this working for you in these areas of your life?

Physically

Mentally

Emotionally

Spiritually

How is this <u>not</u> working for you in these areas of your life?

Physically

Mentally

Emotionally

Spiritually

Do your actions and beliefs in this area align with your current values?

Which SELF sub-personality parts are showing up for you?

How are these parts holding you back right now?

How are these actions or beliefs impacting this part of the system?

How are these actions or beliefs impacting other parts of the system?

What do you want to <u>stop</u> doing in this area of your life?

What do you want to <u>start</u> doing in this area of your life?

What do you want to <u>continue</u> doing in this area of your life?

Future

What do you want this area of your life to look like?

In a perfect world, how would it feel?

What questions do you still have about this area of your life?

How would a change impact your life, for better or for worse?

Personal Identity System
Foundational | Soul

Answer the self-reflections questions below as they relate to the **Personal Identity Priorities** you listed above.

PERSONAL IDENTITY SYSTEM: *Copy your top priority from above.*

Past

What actions or beliefs seem to be a pattern in this area of your life?

How did these beliefs or patterns become a part of your routine?

_____

_____

_____

_____

_____

_____

_____

_____

What benefits were you getting from this behavior then? How was it serving you?

_____

_____

_____

_____

_____

_____

_____

_____

Present

What are you getting from this now?

_____

_____

_____

_____

_____

_____

How has this become a habit for you, in your current life? How does it manifest now?

_____

_____

_____

_____

_____

How is this working for you in these areas of your life?

Physically

_____

_____

_____

_____

_____

Mentally

_____

_____

_____

_____

_____

Emotionally

_____

_____

_____

_____

_____

Spiritually

_____
_____
_____
_____
_____

How is this <u>not</u> working for you in these areas of your life?

Physically

_____
_____
_____
_____
_____

Mentally

_____
_____
_____
_____
_____

Emotionally

_____
_____
_____
_____
_____

Spiritually

Do your actions and beliefs in this area align with your current values?

Which SELF sub-personality parts are showing up for you?

How are these parts holding you back right now?

How are these actions or beliefs impacting this part of the system?

_____

_____

_____

_____

_____

How are these actions or beliefs impacting other parts of the system?

_____

_____

_____

_____

_____

What do you want to <u>stop</u> doing in this area of your life?

_____

_____

_____

_____

_____

What do you want to <u>start</u> doing in this area of your life?

_____

_____

_____

_____

_____

What do you want to <u>continue</u> doing in this area of your life?

Future

What do you want this area of your life to look like?

In a perfect world, how would it feel?

What questions do you still have about this area of your life?

How would a change impact your life, for better or for worse?

NEXT STEPS

A huge part of the **Evaluate** stage is to acknowledge the grief, loss, and fear that may come up as you consider moving forward in different areas of your life. Transition is one of the hardest things we confront as humans. We're wired for certainty and consistency. Our survival instincts kick in when we face new experiences. Sometimes that means our emotions become overwhelming, which can easily make us abandon all of these positive changes we're making. Even the idea of change can be so fear-inducing that we may decide our current reality, however terrible it is, is better than the unknown.

Taking this step to acknowledge the areas of your life is a huge step forward. Take a little time to celebrate all of the work you've done so far. You're on the path to a Whole SELF Lifestyle!

BONUS RECAP

You can find these bonus materials in our **Bonus Library** at: www. wholeselflifestyle.com/working-parents/bonus-library.

- **Evaluation Checklist**

9

STEP 3: (L) LIST OF SOLUTIONS

The third step in the Whole SELF Lifestyle framework is "**L**," for **List of Solutions**. Now that you've identified the different elements of the systems of your life and have analyzed how those areas are functioning for *you*, it's time to start identifying the *actions* you'll implement in your daily life to make improvements. You won't be making all of these changes right now. In fact, you won't be making *any* changes quite yet. Right now, we're just going to create a comprehensive list of action steps you *could* take to enhance the quality of your life. For now, just get everything out on paper, and then at the end we'll identify the best solution(s) to implement.

---

66 *Rather than looking at information as holding the answers, I implore you to look at information as giving you the tools to find the answers yourself.* -Pia Silva

---

SELF-REFLECTION QUESTIONS

Answer the self-reflections questions below as they relate to the **3 priorities** you listed in the last chapter.

LIFE MANAGEMENT SYSTEM: *Copy your priority here for easy reference.*

_____
_____
_____

What do you **already know** about improving this area of your life?

_____
_____
_____
_____
_____
_____
_____

What **past experience** or **knowledge** can you call upon now to make changes right away, without doing any other research or learning?

_____
_____
_____
_____
_____
_____
_____

What do you just need to **implement** right now? What do you know you need to **start** doing immediately? Does anything come to mind?

What **assumptions** are you making about changing this part of your life?

What **resistance** are you facing in changing this part of your life? What are you **afraid** will happen if you succeed in improving this area of your life?

What **information** are you **missing** right now? What do you
need to **learn** in order to make changes in this area of your life?

_____
_____
_____
_____
_____
_____

Which of the following resources do you want to follow up on to fill
in gaps in knowledge or to brainstorm new ideas? Specify what you'd
like to do in each area: **Google, Articles, Podcasts, Books,
Conferences & Classes, Friends & Family, Social Media,
Parenting Groups, Professional Contacts, Doctors,
Therapist, Coach, Other**.

_____
_____
_____
_____
_____
_____
_____
_____
_____
_____
_____
_____
_____
_____

EMOTIONAL INTELLIGENCE SYSTEM: *Copy your priority here for easy reference.*

_____

_____

_____

What do you **already know** about improving this area of your life?

_____

_____

_____

_____

_____

_____

_____

_____

_____

What **past experience** or **knowledge** can you call upon now to make changes right away, without doing any other research or learning?

_____

_____

_____

_____

_____

_____

_____

_____

What do you just need to **implement** right now? What do you know you need to **start** doing immediately? Does anything come to mind?

_____
_____
_____
_____
_____
_____

What **assumptions** are you making about changing this part of your life?

_____
_____
_____
_____
_____
_____

What **resistance** are you facing in changing this part of your life? What are you **afraid** will happen if you succeed in improving this area of your life?

_____
_____
_____
_____
_____
_____
_____
_____

What **information** are you **missing** right now? What do you need to **learn** in order to make changes in this area of your life?

Which of the following resources do you want to follow up on to fill in gaps in knowledge or to brainstorm new ideas? Specify what you'd like to do in each area: **Google, Articles, Podcasts, Books, Conferences & Classes, Friends & Family, Social Media, Parenting Groups, Professional Contacts, Doctors, Therapist, Coach, Other**.

PERSONAL IDENTITY SYSTEM: *Copy your priority here for easy reference.*

_____
_____
_____

What do you **already know** about improving this area of your life?

_____
_____
_____
_____
_____
_____
_____
_____

What **past experience** or **knowledge** can you call upon now to make changes right away, without doing any other research or learning?

_____
_____
_____
_____
_____
_____
_____

What do you just need to **implement** right now? What do you know you need to **start** doing immediately? Does anything come to mind?

What **assumptions** are you making about changing this part of your life?

What **resistance** are you facing in changing this part of your life? What are you **afraid** will happen if you succeed in improving this area of your life?

What **information** are you **missing** right now? What do you need to **learn** in order to make changes in this area of your life?

Which of the following resources do you want to follow up on to fill in gaps in knowledge or to brainstorm new ideas? Specify what you'd like to do in each area: **Google, Articles, Podcasts, Books, Conferences & Classes, Friends & Family, Social Media, Parenting Groups, Professional Contacts, Doctors, Therapist, Coach, Other**.

MASTER LIST OF ACTION STEPS

Now that you've gone through your analysis and have done some research, create a list of *all* of the possible action steps you can take to improve each area of your life. This is your master list of action steps you *could* implement, based on what you know now. Make your list for *every* area before you start making any decisions, as there might be some overlap.

Try to come up with at least ten ideas for each area, but keep adding as many as you need. Also feel free to come back and update these lists whenever you need to. This can be a living document to pull from.

LIFE MANAGEMENT SYSTEM: *Copy your priority here for easy reference.*

What **specific action steps** could you *potentially* take to improve this area of your life. Include as **many ideas** as you can. Break each idea down to the **smallest** action step possible.

EMOTIONAL INTELLIGENCE SYSTEM: *Copy your priority here for easy reference.*

_____
_____
_____

What **specific action steps** could you *potentially* take to improve this area of your life. Include as **many ideas** as you can. Break each idea down to the **smallest** action step possible.

_____
_____
_____
_____
_____
_____
_____
_____
_____
_____
_____
_____
_____
_____
_____
_____
_____
_____
_____

PERSONAL IDENTITY SYSTEM: *Copy your priority here for easy reference.*

What **specific action steps** could you *potentially* take to improve this area of your life. Include as **many ideas** as you can. Break each idea down to the **smallest** action step possible.

———

*You can access the **List of Solutions Checklist** in the **Bonus Library*** at: *www.wholeselflifestyle.com/working-parents/bonus-library.*

———

COMMITMENTS

Now it's time to make some decisions! You should have a wide range of different solutions you can implement in order to improve the various areas of your life. Answer these questions to identify the action steps that make the most sense to implement *right now*. You'll eliminate some options, and you'll set some others aside for now - that's okay. The point here is to come up with a short list of actions you can integrate into your daily life now, without sacrificing the other areas of your life.

Which of these action steps seem the **most doable** right now?

Which of these action steps seem **impossible** for me right now?

_____

_____

_____

_____

_____

_____

_____

_____

_____

_____

_____

_____

_____

Which of these action steps seem **fun** and **enjoyable** to implement?

_____

_____

_____

_____

_____

_____

_____

_____

_____

_____

_____

_____

_____

Which of these action steps feel **exhausting** to even think about doing?

Which of these action steps am I **avoiding** because I'm afraid? Is there a way to overcome this fear?

Which of these action steps would make the biggest positive impact in ***this*** **area** of my life?

Which of these action steps would make the biggest positive impact in the ***other*** **areas** of my life?

Which of these action steps would **negatively impact** the other areas of my life?

Which of these action steps would make **other options easier to implement** later if I do this now?

———

*You can access the **Commitment Checklist** in the **Bonus Library** at: www.wholeselflifestyle.com/working-parents/bonus-library.*

———

SETTING YOURSELF UP FOR SUCCESS

You can go through the entire Whole SELF Lifestyle process without ever seeing results if you don't make a commitment to follow through with actions. It's incredibly tempting to keep doing research to avoid really making changes in your life. But all the knowledge and insights in the world are just entertainment if you don't *do* anything with that information. Taking action is where the rubber really meets the road.

The next step of the Whole SELF Lifestyle is all about experimenting with new actions in your life: new skills, new habits, new routines, new processes, new boundaries, new conversations. Take this opportunity to choose which actions you are ready to take now. In the next chapter, you'll craft a plan to make it happen.

What actions are you **committed** to doing in this area of your life now? Start **small** and **simple**.

_____
_____
_____
_____
_____
_____

How are you going to take this action? What does it look like? Be specific.

_____
_____
_____
_____
_____
_____

When are you going to take this action? How will this fit into your **current routine**?

What are you going to **stop** doing in your life? How will you **eliminate** that action from your life?

What will **prevent** you from taking this action? What will make it **difficult** to follow through?

How can you **plan ahead** now to prevent likely obstacles or challenges?

_____
_____
_____
_____
_____
_____
_____

It's easier to replace habits than it is to introduce or remove them in your life. What unhealthy habit(s) can you **replace** right now? What **new habit** will you replace that habit with?

_____
_____
_____
_____
_____
_____
_____

How can you set yourself up for **success**? What needs to change in your **environment**, **routine** or **relationships** to ensure you stay on track?

_____
_____
_____
_____
_____
_____
_____

How can you prevent **excuses** or **procrastination** from holding you back?

_____
_____
_____
_____
_____
_____

What can you do when things get **uncomfortable** or **scary**? Who can you reach out to for support in those challenging moments?

_____
_____
_____
_____
_____
_____

———

BONUS RECAP

You can find these bonus materials in our **Bonus Library** at: www.wholeselflifestyle.com/working-parents/bonus-library.

- **List of Solutions Checklist**
- **Commitment Checklist**

10

STEP 4: (F) FAMILIARIZE

The fourth and final step of the Whole SELF Lifestyle framework is "**F**," for **Familiarize**. This step is often the hardest part of the Whole SELF Lifestyle for working parents, but it's also the most critical. The other three steps will give you a clear and customized roadmap to follow to improve the different systems in your life. But so far, your roadmap is still just a theory. This is the step where you *finally* get to implement all of your great plans to experience the Whole SELF Lifestyle for yourself. This step is all about gathering feedback about what *actually* works for you in your unique life, and what doesn't. This step is all about familiarizing yourself with new skills, new beliefs, new ways of being, a whole new lifestyle - one that does *not* include burnout, resentment, and frustration.

In the last step, you identified a list of action steps you are committed to taking in different areas of your life. Now it's time to go for it! Start experimenting. Try things out. Start small. Keep things simple. Do something you know will work first, so you can experience some early success and stay motivated to continue. Stay flexible. Adapt. Adjust things if they're not working. Be honest with yourself.

Let go of outside pressure or opinions and look *within yourself* for answers. Listen to your intuition. See where this path takes you.

The key is to *stay observant*. There's no such thing as failure in this phase - just feedback. Take notes about what's working for you and what's not. Don't force things that simply aren't working, but don't give up too soon either. There's a sweet spot in personal growth, and this phase is all about learning what that sweet spot is for *you*. Here are some self-reflection questions to help you discover your own personal sweet spot.

———

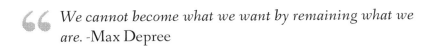 *We cannot become what we want by remaining what we are.* -Max Depree

———

SELF-REFLECTION QUESTIONS

Answer the self-reflections questions below as they relate to each **action step** you take.

What did I **learn** from implementing this action step?

Which actions felt **easy** and **light**? Which actions felt **forced** or **stressful**?

Which action steps **contributed** to my energy levels? Which ones **depleted** my energy?

How does this make me **feel today**? How have I felt over the last week as I've integrated this into my life?

What do I need to do **more** of? **Less** of?

_____

_____

_____

_____

_____

_____

_____

_____

Do I feel like my daily life is more in **alignment** with my **values**, or am I moving away from my values?

_____

_____

_____

_____

_____

_____

_____

What have I been too **afraid** to try? What's **holding me back** right now?

_____

_____

_____

_____

_____

_____

_____

_____

Where have I fallen back into **old patterns** and **behaviors**? What triggered that backslide?

What has been **too big** a change, too soon? Where do I need to take a step back?

What are my most common **barriers to growth**? How do those barriers manifest in my daily life? What does it *look* and *feel* like for me?

How has my life changed, for **better** and **worse**, since I started doing this?

Which **skills** do I still need to develop? What's my **next step** in getting what I need?

———

*You can also access the **Keep It Or Drop It Checklist** in the **Bonus Library** at: www.wholeselflifestyle.com/working-parents/ bonus-library.*

———

*You can also access the **How to Say No Gracefully** in the **Bonus Library** at: www.wholeselflifestyle.com/working-parents/bonus-library.*

———

NEXT STEPS

This step is all about taking action so you can gain real-world self-discovery. Not every option you came up with in the last step is going to be feasible or even preferable to follow through on. Some options might be great to try now. Other options might be a great fit in the future, but not now. So pick and choose the options that are best for *you, your* family, *your* career, and *your* life, right now.

Don't try to make too many changes all at once. Take your time. Let new practices and perspectives sink in before switching it up again. Breathe through the discomfort and reach out for support from your circle of influence when you need it (more on this in the next chapter).

Over time, you'll familiarize yourself with new ways of being in the world. You'll familiarize yourself with new habits and new routines. You'll familiarize yourself with how *you*, as a unique individual, personally react to certain behaviors, thoughts, and feelings. You'll familiarize yourself with your limits and your preferences. You'll discover what *gives* you energy and what *depletes* your energy. You'll discover what works for *you*, in this moment, under *these circumstances*. Through this process, you'll start to see different aspects of your life shift and improve, and you'll have the self-knowledge to know how to respond to those changes. Eventually, you'll realize that you're truly living a Whole SELF Lifestyle.

———

BONUS RECAP

You can find these bonus materials in our **Bonus Library** at: www.wholeselflifestyle.com/working-parents/bonus-library.

- **Keep It or Drop It Checklist**
- **How to Say No Gracefully**

11

BUILDING YOUR CIRCLE OF INFLUENCE

Building a solid support system is one of the most important and effective things you can do when you start prioritizing balance over burnout. You don't exist in a vacuum, and it's important to have people on your side as you begin to improve your life.

This chapter will help you identify those people in your life who are the most likely to support, encourage, and inspire you to continue this journey when things get difficult. These are the people who are as interested in your best interests as their own. They can be trusted to walk with you through this transition in your life. Not all relationships are created equal, and the best way to set yourself up for success is to surround yourself with people who will support your progress.

As you are shifting, you will begin to realize that you are not the same person you used to be. The things you used to tolerate have become intolerable. When you once remained quiet, you are now speaking your truth. You are beginning to understand the value of your voice and there are some situations that no longer deserve your time, energy, and focus. -Mindset of Greatness

SUPPORT TO SEEK

List the names of anyone in your life who meets the description in each of the following statements. You can list just one person, or many. You can also name the same person for more than one statement. The more people you can think of the better, but don't add them just to have a lot of people on your list. They should meet this criterion completely and consistently.

- I feel comfortable being myself around them.
- I can be honest with them without being afraid of their reaction.
- I can be vulnerable and emotional with them without worrying about being judged.
- They are genuinely happy for me when I succeed or have good news.
- They offer sound advice and show good judgment in their life.
- They are honest with me when they think I'm on the wrong track.
- They encourage me to make my own decisions without influencing the outcome.
- They have achieved something in their life that I would like to achieve.
- They are kind and courteous to me and others in their life.

- There is no drama in our relationship. Disagreements are handled with respect.
- They are reliable. I can count on them to be there for me when I need them.
- They can be trusted to keep our conversations confidential. They don't gossip.
- I feel inspired to be a better person when they're around.
- I feel comfortable sharing my wins AND my failures with them.

SUPPORT TO AVOID

Not every relationship is supportive, even if it appears to be on the surface. Here are some clues that someone should *not* be a source of support as you make significant changes in your life. You don't have to exclude these people from your life altogether, but you may not want to go directly to these people as you integrate new changes in your life. Their response could have a negative impact on your overall growth. List the names of anyone in your life who meets the description in each of the following statements.

- They can be critical and judgmental.
- They tend to put my ideas down or ridicule me.
- They sometimes talk about other people behind their back.
- They have some incentive to keep me from changing (boss, spouse, parent, etc.).
- They complain without taking action to change the circumstances in their life.
- They don't understand why I would want to work so hard to change this part of my life.

- I'm not sure how they would react to my sharing "big" feelings.
- Our relationship is based more on my helping them than the other way around. There's a lack of reciprocation.
- They don't really have any experience or practical insights about this particular area I'm trying to improve.

———

CIRCLE OF INFLUENCE

You should now have a short list of people you can go to for support and advice. Make a note of these peoples, and the areas where they might be able to provide the most support for you. This is your Circle of Influence. These are the best people to seek out when you need encouragement or guidance as you make changes in your life.

———

*You can access the **Circle of Influence Checklist** in the **Bonus Library** at: www.wholeselflifestyle.com/working-parents/bonus-library.*

———

BONUS RECAP

You can find these bonus materials in our **Bonus Library** at: www.wholeselflifestyle.com/working-parents/bonus-library.

- **Circle of Influence Checklist**

PART III

12

LIVING A WHOLE SELF LIFESTYLE

Now that you've gone through the entire Whole SELF Lifestyle process, the key is to continue implementing it throughout your life. Again, this is a *lifestyle*. This isn't a one-time fix. The more you explore these questions, the more deeply you'll know and understand yourself. Over time, you won't have to write the answers out, although you always can. Your instincts will take over and you'll start asking these questions in the moment, which can prevent you from getting pulled off course in your life. Use the Whole SELF Lifestyle as a tool to enhance your life... not only in the individual areas of your life, but as a *whole*.

Change is not a bolt of lightning that arrives with a zap. It is a bridge, built brick by brick, every day, with sweat, humanity, and slips. It is hard work, and slow work, but it can be thrilling to watch it take shape. -Sarah Hepola

------

WHEN TO IMPLEMENT THE WHOLE SELF LIFESTYLE

There will be a tendency to go through this process once, and then move on to the next bright and shiny self-help book. This book is designed to help you not just once, but on an *ongoing* basis. These exercises are here for you whenever you need them. Here are some specific circumstances under which the Whole SELF Lifestyle process can be particularly helpful.

RESTORATIVE CHECK-IN

You can go through the Whole SELF Lifestyle framework when you're struggling with burnout and need to escape survival mode. This is what I call a **Restorative Check-In**.

- When you're feeling **resentful** or **over-burdened**.
- When you're **physically sick**, **tired**, or when your health is failing.
- When you're facing or are in the midst of a **major life change**, like moving, changing jobs, or welcoming a new baby into your family (or, you know, dealing with the aftermath of a once-in-a-lifetime pandemic).
- When a part of **any of your systems shift** and change. This is a good time to determine what adjustments might need to be made to the whole ecosystem.
- When a part of **any of your systems aren't working**. When you're feeling unfulfilled in any particular area of your life, either externally, internally, or on a fundamental level.

- When you find yourself **blaming others** for your life circumstances. Feeling like a victim or a martyr is a big sign that it's time to reclaim your power by going through this process.
- When you're feeling a sense of **failure**, **guilt**, like you're **settling**, or like you're not meeting your potential in a certain area of your life.
- When you're **comparing yourself to others**.
- When you **find yourself trying to "fix" or change other people** in order to solve your problems.
- When you're dealing with **overwhelm**, **anxiety**, **sadness**, **anger**, or any other intense emotions, and can't see a way out.

———

*You can also access the **Restorative Check-In** in the **Bonus Library** at: www.wholeselflifestyle.com/working-parents/bonus-library.*

———

PREVENTATIVE CHECK-IN

You can also set aside time on a daily or weekly or another regular basis to run through this simplified list of questions as part of your personal self-care process. This would be a **Preventative Check-In**.

What did I **learn** today?

_____

_____

What activities felt **easy** and **light**? Which activities felt **forced** or **stressful**?

Which activities **contributed** to my energy levels? Which ones **depleted** my energy?

Which relationships **filled me up** today? Which relationships made me **feel badly about myself** today?

How do I **feel today**? How have I felt over the **last week**? Over the last **month**?

What do I need to do **more** of? **Less** of?

Do I feel like my daily life is more in **alignment** with my **values**, or am I moving away from my values?

———

*You can also access the **Preventative Check-In** in the **Bonus Library** at: www.wholeselflifestyle.com/working-parents/bonus-library.*

———

BONUS RECAP

You can find these bonus materials in our **Bonus Library** at: www.wholeselflifestyle.com/working-parents/bonus-library.

- **Restorative Check-In**
- **Preventative Check-In**

13

HOW TO AVOID A RELAPSE INTO BURNOUT?

Now that you're familiar with the Whole SELF Lifestyle, there are a number of ways you can go even deeper to integrate this practice into your daily life. Through your actions, you can also start to spread a new message that working parenthood doesn't need to be a miserable and exhausting experience. It's time for us to create a new lifestyle for working parents that is understanding, fulfilling, and allows each person to live the life that's most effective for them. Broad cultural adoption of this new lifestyle starts with *you*.

---

66 *Owning our story and loving ourselves through that process is the bravest thing that we'll ever do.* -Brene Brown, Ph.D., LCSW

HOW TO MAINTAIN THESE CHANGES

Here are a number of recommendations to help you integrate the changes you've made into your life in deeper and new ways. Pick and choose any of these options, depending on your needs. Come back to this list often and keep trying new things. Discover what works best for *you*.

1. **Refer to *The Whole SELF Lifestyle for Working Parents* book** whenever you need a little life upgrade... in a *single* area of your life, or in *all* areas of your life. Use the framework whenever you need guidance or are feeling burned out.

2. **Integrate these activities into your daily routine.** Use the **Bonus Library** materials to enhance your life experiences and relationships.

3. **Use this Companion Workbook** for ongoing support. Refer to those exercises whenever you need to get back on track.

4. **Go through the Whole SELF Lifestyle framework with your spouse, partner, or family**. Share your answers and brainstorm ways to integrate what you learn into your marriage, your parenting, and your family experience.

5. **Integrate this into the work you're doing with your therapist, coach, or mentor.** Use your responses to these exercises as areas to address your particular challenges and needs in more depth.

6. **Start a Book Club or Whole SELF Lifestyle™ Circle** with your friends or colleagues. Go through the exercises together and discuss your responses with a supportive group. Try this once, or schedule regular check-ins to stay on track.

7. **Listen to the Working Parent Resource**

Podcast to explore all of the topics we discuss here in more depth, and to receive updated information on the Whole SELF Lifestyle. You can listen at www.argenalinstitute.com/podcast, or on all of the major listening apps such as Apple Podcasts, Stitcher, Spotify, Google Play, and iHeartRadio.

8. **Connect with me on social media** to keep the conversation going. My favorite place to connect is on LinkedIn.

9. **Interview me for your podcast, show or article.** Spread the word about the Whole SELF Lifestyle to your friends, clients, co-workers, and community. Visit www.wholeselflifestyle.com/working-parents/consultation to schedule a **free consultation** with me to discuss further.

10. **Apply to work with me privately, either individually or in one of my group programs or events**. Dive deeper and receive personalized support. Visit www.wholeselflifestyle.com/working-parents/consultation to schedule a **free consultation** with me to discuss further.

11. **Integrate the Whole SELF Lifestyle framework in the following group settings**. Visit www.wholeselflifestyle.com/working-parents/consultation to schedule a **free consultation** with me to discuss further.

- Company Training
- Parenting Groups
- Association Meetings
- Industry Events
- Conferences

- Wellness Retreats
- High schools and Universities
- Business and Graduate Schools
- Non-Profit Institutions

14

A NEW FUTURE

The pervasive feelings of stress, hopelessness, and burnout in our society won't change until we become healthier ourselves. We must get our own house in order before we will ever be strong enough to help anyone else. As we integrate the principles of the Whole SELF Lifestyle into our own lives, we'll become equipped to improve our reality, as well as that of the people around us.

That said, becoming self-aware isn't all about prioritizing *self* over the collective at all costs. Being a positive member of society involves keeping the fate of the community in mind. When we have a robust sense of self, we naturally embrace the compassion, empathy, and motivation necessary for a healthy and supportive society. The Whole SELF Lifestyle starts within, but it doesn't end there. As you integrate the Whole SELF Lifestyle into your daily life, here are a few other ways you can improve not only your own life, but the world around you too:

- As you explore the depths of your identity, you'll be more prepared to leverage that unique mix of qualities only *you* have to improve your world - at home, at work, and everywhere in between.

- You can eliminate that fractured feeling that comes from trying to be too many things to too many people in too many different situations. You'll redistribute all of that energy back to yourself. You'll start to operate more deliberately from a deeper sense of self and purpose. That allows you to offer the best of yourself to the people around you. As you become healthier, you'll naturally become a better partner, parent, friend, and member of your community.

- You'll replace that impulse to find a quick fix with a more comprehensive perspective of your life. You'll begin to see personal development as an ongoing, messy, but ultimately far more fulfilling practice that leads to a healthier and happier lifestyle.

- You'll return to having real connection and intimacy in your relationships - at home, at work, and in society in general. You'll encounter less conflict and more understanding within your family, in the workplace, and in your community.

- You'll leverage the vast array of information that exists out there in an *intentional* way, rather than feeling bombarded by information, opinions, and advice. You can reject the "guru culture" that can be so tempting and start trusting your internal wisdom. Your instincts and your values will be your guide as you pick and choose the advice that's best for you and your family.

- You can opt out of measuring your self-worth by other people's definitions and expectations. You can refer to your deepest values as your true North Star.

- You don't have to numb out in your life anymore. You don't have to try to avoid the painful parts of life. Instead, you can use your valuable time to recharge, fill your cup, and experience more meaningful moments.

- You can let go of the fear, anxiety, and paralysis that comes with uncertainty. You can start to embrace life as it comes because you'll trust you have the tools and skills to handle whatever comes at you. You'll see challenges as opportunities for personal growth. You'll see a conflict with others as a way to not only strengthen your relationship but as a way to become an even better version of yourself.

- Together we can increase tolerance and inclusion for all walks of life in our communities as we embrace each other's differences, unique qualities and gifts. As we come to know, love, and accept our full selves, it's much easier to do the same for others.

- You can look back on your life with no regrets. The Whole SELF Lifestyle™ allows you to soak in those precious moments with your kids when they're little, build a stable and loving partnership with your spouse, and take care of yourself in each moment.

Self-awareness isn't a requirement to *survive* your life, but it *is* a requirement to *enjoy* your life. The more you know yourself, the more you'll enjoy this adventure called working parenthood. I hope the Whole SELF Lifestyle offers the inspiration and structure to help you kick off your own journey of self-discovery.

———

66 *Life balance is about creating a life that flows with you rather than a life you have to power through.* -Jaime Marie Wilson

———

ENJOY THESE PRECIOUS YEARS OF YOUR LIFE

At the end of our lives, all we have is our relationships and our memories. It's easy to take these early years of working parenthood for granted. The chaos of life with kids can feel so demanding and tedious. Changing diapers. Responding to our two hundredth work email of the day. Cooking another dinner, which will probably go uneaten by picky kids. Folding the 3,439th load of laundry. The days can feel like a nonstop grind.

There will be a day in your not too distant future when you'll look back at *this moment* of your life and you'll remember... *something*. My hope is that you'll look back with fond memories of the giggles, the conversations, and the cuddles. I want you to look back with the certainty that you made the *most* of these moments, because the only thing we know for certain right now is soon those moments *will* be gone. I hope you'll pause in those moments of chaos and prioritize love and connection. I invite you to *choose* the life you *want*, over the life you feel you're required to tolerate. Will there be bad days? Of course, that's part of life. But only *you* are in a position to ensure the heartwarming experiences outnumber the tiresome ones. Reclaim that power for yourself today. Remind yourself of your power often.

I challenge you to release old notions of work-life balance, and instead embrace the Whole SELF Lifestyle as an intentional practice in your life as a working parent. I invite you to *enjoy* these precious years with your family. Take this opportunity to foster the memories and the relationships that will live in your heart today, at the end of your life, and every day in between.

APPENDIX

RECOMMENDED RESOURCES

APPENDIX 1

These Recommended Resources have been added to the Bonus Library. That version may be updated over time with additional resources, so there may be some minor differences in the list you see in the Bonus Library.

BOOKS

- Alcorn, K. 2013. Maxed Out: American Moms on the Brink. New York, NY: Seal Press.
- Brown, B. 2010. The Gifts of Imperfection: Let Go of Who You Think You're Supposed to Be and Embrace Who You Are. Center City, MN: Hazelden Publishing.
- Burke Harris, Dr. N. 2020. The Deepest Well: Healing the Long-Term Effects of Childhood.
- Denworth, L. (2020, January 28). Friendship: The Evolution, Biology, and Extraordinary Power of Life's Fundamental Bond. New York, NY: W. W. Norton & Company.
- Adversity. London, United Kingdom: Bluebird Books.

- Eyal, N. (2019, September 10). Indistractable: How to Control Your Attention and Choose Your Life. Dallas, TX: BenBella Books.
- Gladwell, M. 2008. Outliers: The Story of Success. New York, NY: Hachette Book Group.
- Gottman, J., Schwartz Gottman, J. 2007. And Baby Makes Three: The Six-Step Plan for Preserving Marital Intimacy and Rekindling Romance After Baby Arrives. New York, NY: Harmony Books.
- Huffington, A. 2014. Thrive: The Third Metric to Redefining Success and Creating a Life of Well-Being, Wisdom, and Wonder. New York, NY: Harmony Books.
- Manne, K. 2017. Down Girl: The Logic of Misogyny. Cary, NC: Oxford University Press.
- Markham, L. 2012. Peaceful Parent, Happy Kids: How to Stop Yelling and Start Connecting. London, United Kingdom: Penguin Group.
- McKeown, G. 2014. Essentialism: The Disciplined Pursuit of Less. New York, NY: Random House LLC.
- McNamee, R. 2019. Zucked: Waking Up to the Facebook Catastrophe. London, United Kingdom: Penguin Group.
- Newport, C. (2019, February 5). Digital Minimalism: Choosing a Focused Life in a Noisy World. London, United Kingdom: Penguin Group (USA) LLC.
- Nichols, T. (2018, October 1). The Death of Expertise: The Campaign against Established Knowledge and Why it Matters. Oxford, England, UK: Oxford University Press.
- Rodsky, E. (2019, October 1). Fair Play: A Game-Changing Solution for When You Have Too Much to Do (and More Life to Live). New York, NY: G.P. Putnam's Sons.

- Sandberg, S. 2013. Lean In: Women, Work, and the Will to Lead. New York, NY: Random House LLC.
- Siegel , D., Payne Bryson, T. 2011. The Whole Brain Child: 12 Revolutionary Strategies to Nurture Your Child's Developing Mind. New York, NY: Delacorte Press.
- Stoddard, J. 2020. Be Mighty: A Woman's Guide to Liberation from Anxiety, Worry, and Stress Using Mindfulness and Acceptance. Oakland, CA: New Harbinger Publications.
- Stromberg, L. 2019. Work, Pause, Thrive: How to Pause for Parenthood Without Ruining Your Career. Dallas, TX: BenBella Books.
- Tsabary, S. 2010. The Conscious Parent: Transforming Ourselves, Empowering Our Children. Vancouver, Canada: Namaste Publishing.
- Zuckerman, E. 2013. Digital Cosmopolitans: Why We Think the Internet Connects Us, Why It Doesn't, and How to Rewire It. New York, NY: W. W. Norton & Company.

ARTICLES & REPORTS

- Arends, B. (2019, April 22). Why the Middle Class is Shrinking. *Market Watch*. Retrieved from https://www.marketwatch.com/story/why-the-middle-class-is-shrinking-2019-04-12
- Argenal, S. (2019, December 9). 3 Skills that Help Me Navigate Working Parenthood. *Healthline*. Retrieved from https://www.healthline.com/health/parenting/3-surprising-skills-that-help-me-navigate-working-parenthood
- Argenal, S. (2019, June 26). Why Focusing on Self-Care Isn't Fixing Burnout for Working Parents. *Working*

Mother. Retrieved from https://www.workingmother. com/why-focusing-on-self-care-isnt-fixing-burnout-for-working-moms

- Baer, D. (2014, July 3). New Study Destroys Malcolm Gladwell's 10,000 Hour Rule. *Business Insider*. Retrieved from https://www.businessinsider.com/new-study-destroys-malcolm-gladwells-10000-rule-2014-7
- Burn-out an 'Occupational Phenomenon': International Classification of Diseases. (2019, May 28). *World Health Organization*. Retrieved from https://www.who.int/ mental_health/evidence/burn-out/en/
- Carrell, R. (2019, August 15). Let's Share Women's Mental Load. *Forbes*. Retrieved from https://www. forbes.com/sites/rachelcarrell/2019/08/15/lets-share-womens-mental-load/#52b95a566bd6
- Casselman, B. (2019, May 2). Why Wages Are Finally Rising, 10 Years After the Recession. *The New York Times*. Retrieved from https://www.nytimes.com/2019/ 05/02/business/economy/wage-growth-economy.html
- Desilver, D. (2018, August 7). For Most U.S. Workers, Real Wages Have Barely Budged in Decades. *Pew Research Center*. Retrieved from https://www. pewresearch.org/fact-tank/2018/08/07/for-most-us-workers-real-wages-have-barely-budged-for-decades/
- Downey, M. (2020 April 1). This is Not Home Schooling, Distance Learning or Online Schooling. *Atlanta Journal Constitution*. Retrieved from https:// www.ajc.com/blog/get-schooled/opinion-this-not-home-schooling-distance-learning-online-schooling/ b9rNnK77eyVLhsRMhaqZwL/amp.html
- Facts & Statistics. (n.d.). *Anxiety and Depression Association of America*. Retrieved from https://adaa.org/ about-adaa/press-room/facts-statistics
- Facts About Bullying (n.d.). *Stop Bullying*. Retrieved

from https://www.stopbullying.gov/media/facts/index.html

- Fox, M. (2018, May 10). Major Depression on the Rise Among Everyone, New Data Shows. *NBC News.* Retrieved from https://www.nbcnews.com/health/health-news/major-depression-rise-among-everyone-new-data-shows-n873146

- Francis, L. (2019, December 13). Dads Are Experiencing the Motherhood Penalty. That's Not Good. *Fatherly.* Retrieved from https://www.fatherly.com/love-money/relationships/motherhood-penalty-dads/

- Friedman, Z. (2019, January 11). 78% of Workers Live Paycheck to Paycheck. *Forbes.* Retrieved from https://www.forbes.com/sites/zackfriedman/2019/01/11/live-paycheck-to-paycheck-government-shutdown/#5040a5ac4f10

- Fuller, J., Manjari, R. (2019, January 17). The Caring Company. *Harvard Business Review.* Retrieved from https://www.hbs.edu/managing-the-future-of-work/Documents/The_Caring_Company.pdf

- Garcia-Alonso, J., Krentz, M., Lovich, D., Quickenden, S., Brooks Taplett, F. (2019, April 10). Lightening the Mental Load that Holds Women Back. *Boston Consulting Group.* Retrieved from https://www.bcg.com/publications/2019/lightening-mental-load-holds-women-back.aspx

- Gassam, J. (2019 March 23). Why Leaning In Doesn't Apply to Women of Color. *Forbes.* Retrieved from https://www.forbes.com/sites/janicegassam/2019/03/23/why-leaning-in-has-not-worked-for-women-of-color/

- Henley, D. (2020 February 16). How to Thrive In Complexity and Chaos. *Forbes.* Retrieved from https://www.forbes.com/sites/dedehenley/2020/02/16/

embrace-the-chaos-what-you-can-learn-in-complex-
environments/#22b504b44db9

- Huffington, A. (2019 March 25). The United States of
Stress. *Thrive Global*. Retrieved from https://
thriveglobal.com/stories/stress-crisis-sanjay-gupta-hbo-
united-states/amp/
- Illing, S. (2020, March 7). What We Get Wrong About
Misogyny. *Vox*. Retrieved from https://www.vox.com/
identities/2017/12/5/16705284/metoo-weinstein-
misogyny-trump-sexism
- Jones, M. (2017, October 19). 11 Billion Reasons the
Self-Help Industry Doesn't Want You to Know The
Truth About Happiness. *Inc*. Retrieved from https://
www.inc.com/matthew-jones/11-billion-reasons-self-
help-industry-doesnt-want-you-to-know-truth-about-
happiness.html
- Kindelan, K. (2020 March 26). Women More Stressed,
Burdened by Coronavirus Than Men, Poll Finds. 5 Ways
to Change That. *Good Morning America*. Retrieved from
https://www.goodmorningamerica.com/wellness/story/
women-stressed-burdened-coronavirus-men-poll-finds-
ways-69787591
- Levitin, D. (2015 January 18). Why the Modern World
is Bad For Your Brain. The Guardian. Retrieved from
https://www.theguardian.com/science/2015/jan/18/
modern-world-bad-for-brain-daniel-j-levitin-organized-
mind-information-overload
- Maldonado, Camilo. (2018, July 24). The Cost of
College Increasing Nearly 8 Times Faster than Wages.
Forbes. Retrieved from https://www.forbes.com/sites/
camilomaldonado/2018/07/24/price-of-college-
increasing-almost-8-times-faster-than-
wages/#3bb7f23e66c1
- Morgan, W. V. (2017, September 1). How Social Media

is Killing your Oxytocin Levels and Keeping you from Being your Happiest Self. *Medium*. Retrieved from https://medium.com/@whitneyvmorgan/how-social-media-is-killing-your-oxytocin-levels-and-keeping-you-from-being-your-happiest-self-89e327a375c3

- New Research Shows the 'Mental Load' is Real and Significantly Impacts Working Mothers Both at Home and Work. (2010, October 13). *Business Wire*. Retrieved from https://www.businesswire.com/news/home/20171220005984/en/New-Research-Shows-%E2%80%9CMental-Load%E2%80%9D-Real-Significantly

- Peck, S. (2019 Jan 24). Workplaces Aren't Paying Attention to the Growing Caretaking Crisis, And It's Costing Them Talent. *Forbes*. Retrieved from https://www.forbes.com/sites/sarahkathleenpeck/2019/01/24/workplaces-arent-paying-attention-to-the-growing-caretaking-crisis-and-its-costing-them-talent/?fbclid=IwAR3zDj9X6nozuMAhcahZANUyYD3IGGeo1l1N_71mLM6JoioYc4X5NcabhMo#6e54a5091677

- Reigeluth, C., Bathany, B., Olson, J. (2019, December 2). Comprehensive Systems Design: A New Educational Technology. *NATO Advanced Science Institute Series*. Retrieved from https://link.springer.com/content/pdf/bfm%3A978-3-642-58035-2%2F1.pdf

- Rittenberry, E. (2019, February 1). The American Life is Killing You. *Medium*. Retrieved from https://medium.com/@erikrittenberry/the-american-life-is-killing-you-9e7e68135f4a

- Selingo, J. (2018, June 2). How the Great Recession Changed the Job Market Forever for College Grads. *The Washington Post*. Retrieved from https://www.washingtonpost.com/news/grade-point/wp/2018/06/01/how-the-great-recession-changed-the-job-market-forever-for-college-grads/

- Simmons, M. (2019, January 18). Most People Think This is a Good Habit, But It's Actually Causing Brain Damage. *Mental Model Club*. Retrieved from https://mentalmodelclub.com/mentalmodelclub/junk-learning-billionaire-mind-4.html
- Simon, L. (2018 March 14). How Information Overload Affects the Brain. *PsychCentral*. Retrieved from https://pro.psychcentral.com/how-information-overload-affects-the-brain/
- Simon, M. (2020 March 19). Women and the Hidden Burden of the Coronavirus. *The Hill*. Retrieved from https://thehill.com/changing-america/respect/equality/488509-the-hidden-burden-of-the-coronavirus-on-women
- Skenazy, L., Gray, P. (2020 March 29). Coronavirus is Providing the Course Correction Kids Desperately Needed. *New York Post*. Retrieved from https://nypost.com/2020/03/29/coronavirus-is-providing-the-course-correction-kids-desperately-needed/
- Vox Creative. (2020, February 13). Why You Should Value Privacy, Even If You Have Nothing to Hide. *Vox*. Retrieved from https://www.vox.com/ad/21136449/privacy-data-technology?fbclid=IwAR2WzBQzGKhHGN85vMYkVoWEIKWPGp8sI_DfSxECYa6VbamGYTY9-YZUtuY
- Winerman, Lea. (2019, January). By the Numbers: An Alarming Rise in Suicide. *American Psychological Association*. Retrieved from https://www.apa.org/monitor/2019/01/numbers
- Zalis, S. (2019 February 22). The Motherhood Penalty: Why We're Losing Our Best Talent to Caregiving. *Forbes*. Retrieved from https://www.forbes.com/sites/shelleyzalis/2019/02/22/the-motherhood-penalty-why-were-losing-our-best-talent-to-caregiving/

PODCASTS

- Ables, M., Wilson, A. (Producers). What Fresh Hell [Audio podcast]. Retrieved from https://www.whatfreshhellpodcast.com/
- Argenal, S. (Producer). Working Parent Resource Podcast [Audio podcast]. Retrieved from https://argenalinstitute.com/podcast
- Babauta, L. (Producer). Zen Habits Radio [Audio producer]. Retrieved from http://www.zenhabitsradio.com/
- Brown, B. (Producer). Unlocking Us [Audio podcast]. Retrieved from https://brenebrown.com/podcast/introducing-unlocking-us/
- Chauvin, H. (Producer). The Mom Is In Control Podcast [Audio podcast]. Retrieved from http://heatherchauvin.com/podcast
- Ching, R. (Producer). The Unburdened Life [Audio podcast]. Retrieved from https://www.rebeccaching.com/podcast
- Ellsworth, B. (Producer). Work from Your Happy Place [Audio podcast]. Retrieved from https://www.workfromyourhappyplace.com/podcast/
- Francis, M., Powers, S. (Producers). The Mom Hour [Audio Podcast]. Retrieved from https://themomhour.com/episodes/
- Hennessy, K. (Producer). Mother Like a Boss [Audio podcast]. Retrieved from http://www.kendrahennessy.com/podcast
- Hill, D., Schonbrun, Y., Sorenson, D., Stoddard, J. (Producers). Psychologists Off The Clock [Audio podcast]. Retrieved from https://www.offtheclockpsych.com/episodes
- Koh, C., Dornfest, A. (Producers). The Edit Your Life

Show [Audio podcast]. Retrieved from http://www.edityourlifeshow.com/episodes/

- Lansbury, J. (Producer). Unruffled [Audio podcast]. Retrieved from https://www.janetlansbury.com/podcast-audio/
- Lumanlan, J. (Producer). Your Parenting Mojo Podcast [Audio podcast]. Retrieved from https://yourparentingmojo.com/episodes/
- Marinovich, A. (Producer). Learn with Less [Audio podcast]. Retrieved from https://learnwithless.com/category/podcast/
- Marks, Dr. Tracey (Producer). Beyond Burnout [Audio podcast]. Retrieved from http://beyondburnout.com/category/podcast/
- Shepard, D. (Producer). Armchair Expert [Audio podcast]. Retrieved from https://armchairexpertpod.com/pods
- Silvers, B., Stewart Holland, S. (Producers). The Nuanced Life [Audio podcast]. Retrieved from http://www.pantsuitpoliticsshow.com/blog-tnl

OTHER RESOURCES

- *The Great Hack.* Directed by Karim Amer, Jehane Noujaim, performance by Carole Cadwaddadr, David Carrol, Brittany Kaiser, 2019. *Netflix.* www.thegreathack.com
- Schwartz, Dr. Richard. (n.d.). The Internal Family Systems Model Outline. *IFS Institute.* Retrieved from https://ifs-institute.com/resources/articles/internal-family-systems-model-outline

BONUS LIBRARY INDEX

APPENDIX 2

ACCESS BONUS LIBRARY at: www.wholeselflifestyle.-com/working-parents/bonus-library

Bonus 1 | System Inventory Snapshot

Bonus 2 | Family Management Plan

Bonus 3 | Values & Priorities Profile

Bonus 4 | Evaluate Checklist

Bonus 5 | List of Solutions Checklist

Bonus 6 | Commitment Checklist

Bonus 7 | Keep It or Drop It Checklist

Bonus 8 | How to Say No Gracefully

Bonus 9 | Circle of Influence Checklist

Bonus 10 | Restorative Check-In

Bonus 11 | Preventative Check-In

Bonus 12 | Recommended Resources

ACKNOWLEDGMENTS

I was a teenager the first time I first realized I wanted to write a book. I've had dozens of book ideas in the decades since, but nothing ever felt right. Until now. This book wouldn't exist without the love, guidance, and endless support of a specific group of people.

Mom, you've been by my side in so many important moments of my life, and this is no exception. You cheered me on as I developed the idea for this book, plugged away at the first draft, and polished it until it was a true reflection of what was in my heart. You were the first person I trusted to read this book. Instead of focusing on criticism, you encouraged me to go deeper. You uncovered even more truth, insights and wisdom hidden inside me. This book is significantly better as a result. Thank you for being my guardian angel in so many ways.

To my sister, Emily: you were a seasoned parent long before I became a mom. You offered advice and perspective when I needed it most, but you always encouraged me to trust my instincts, too. You've talked me through my biggest challenges as a working parent. You've been there for me through thick and thin, and I can't imagine life without you. Thank you for holding a mirror up so I could explore my own personal journey of motherhood. I continue to learn so much from you. I am so grateful to have you in my life.

To my Pop Squad: Tracy, Kelly, Kim, Belinda, Anne, and Emily. We left everything we knew when we moved to Austin, and y'all quickly became my Texas family. You bring a smile to my face every day, and it means the world to know you're all there to support me in my lowest moments too. Every working parent should be so lucky to have a crew like ours.

Michelle Mazur: I came to you with a jumble of random concepts and disconnected ideas. You masterfully helped me weave it all together until it made sense. The core of the Whole SELF Lifestyle began with you. You unlocked the conviction I feel about the message in this book and helped me refine my purpose in life. Thank you.

Many thanks to my wonderful editor, Karen Simmering, for your instant response times, your eagle eye, and for bringing this manuscript to life.

Ronald Cruz, thank you so much for designing this book cover. I came to you with a few ideas and some inspiration, and you created something beautiful.

To my podcast guests, who have enriched my knowledge in so many areas of life. Your insights have been invaluable, and your contribution to the world is inspiring. And to my devoted podcast listeners and The Argenal Institute community: you've been on this path of understanding the complexities of working parenthood with me for years now. I can't tell you how much I value the nuance and depth you've contributed to this process.

To my father, siblings, in-laws, and all of my other friends, colleagues, and strangers who have inspired my soul growth along the way. You've made an enormous impact on me, and I appreciate each and every one of you. I hold you all in my heart.

To my boys, Beckett and Weston: you've been my greatest teachers. You made me a mother, and I couldn't be more honored to share this journey in life with you. The purity of your love, the joy in your belly laughs, and the wonder in your eyes makes every day a profound adventure. I am so grateful for you both. Thank you for being my sons.

And finally, to my loving husband, Joey. I don't even know where to begin. This book will be published on the 10th anniversary of the day we met, and you've been by my side ever since. You've supported my wild ideas and my most ambitious dreams. Your commitment, empathy, and love as a husband, father and as a human motivates me to be the best version of myself I can be. Everything that's good in my life starts with you. Thank you for everything you do, and for everything you are.

ABOUT THE AUTHOR

Sarah Argenal, MA, CPC is on a mission to eradicate the burnout epidemic that's crushing working parents so they can finally enjoy these precious years of their lives. She is the founder of The Argenal Institute based in Austin, TX, host of the popular Working Parent Resource Podcast, and creator of the Whole SELF Lifestyle™ Method, a sustainable and long-term approach to personal fulfillment in the modern world.

Sarah combines twenty years of experience in areas such as psychotherapy, professional coaching, teaching, and complex project management to help working parents reclaim their time, energy, and identity. She has been featured in publications such as *NBC News, Healthline, Thrive Global, Working Mother,* and *PsychCentral,* and is a frequent guest on business and parenting podcasts around the world. Sarah lives with her husband and two sons in Austin, Texas. Visit **www.argenalinstitute.com** to learn more.

BEFORE YOU GO

Two final notes before you go.

First, would you mind leaving an honest rating and review on **Amazon**, **Goodreads**, or wherever you bought this book? Your comments would be extremely helpful to other overwhelmed working parents who are trying to decide whether this book might be valuable for them. I would really appreciate your thoughts.

Second, if you would like to stay in touch, receive free resources and tips, and learn more about the various ways I support busy working parents, please visit me at **www.argenalinstitute.com** to learn more, or email me at **hello@argenalinstitute.com** if you'd like to connect. I would love to hear from you!

Made in the USA
Monee, IL
27 April 2021